100 Best Films of the Century

Barry Norman

ORION

First published by Chapmans 1992
This edition first published in 1998 by Orion Media
An imprint of Orion Books Ltd
Orion House
5 Upper St Martin's Lane
London WC2H 9EA

A CIP catalogue record for this book is available from the British Library.

ISBN 0-75281-777-9

Printed and bound in Great Britain by Butler & Tanner, Frome and London

For Samantha and Emma and Piers

Contents

List of Films

The Adventures of Robin Hood
The African Queen
All About Eve
All Quiet on the Western Front
Apocalypse Now
Bad Day at Black Rock
Bambi
The Bank Dick
The Battleship Potemkin
The Best Years of Our Lives
Bicycle Thieves
The Big Sleep
Bonnie and Clyde
Breathless
Bringing up Baby
Butch Cassidy and the Sundance Kid
Cabaret
Casablanca
Chinatown
Citizen Kane
The Discreet Charm of the Bourgeoisie
Double Indemnity
Duck Soup
Les Enfants du Paradis
E.T. – The Extra-Terrestrial
Frankenstein
The General
Genevieve
The Godfather
The Godfather Part II

The Gold Rush
Gone with the Wind
La Grande Illusion
The Grapes of Wrath
Great Expectations
Gregory's Girl
Hannah and Her Sisters
High Noon
His Girl Friday
I Know Where I'm Going
It Happened One Night
It's a Wonderful Life
Les Jeux Interdits
Kind Hearts and Coronets
The Lady Eve
The Lady Vanishes
Laura
The Lavender Hill Mob
Lawrence of Arabia
The Leopard
The Maltese Falcon
M.A.S.H.
A Matter of Life and Death
Mean Streets
Modern Times
My Darling Clementine
Napoleon
Nashville
The Nights of Cabiria
Ninotchka
Oh! Mr Porter
On the Waterfront

Preface

If what you are looking for in the early sections of this book is a detailed history of the cinema you have most certainly come to the wrong place. All I attempt to offer is a quick glide across the first 100 years of what is potentially (and sometimes actually) the most exciting art form of the twentieth century, my purpose being to pick out the most significant developments and thereby give some kind of context to the final section – my choice of the best 100 films of these first 100 years.

Concerning that list there is one thing of which I am quite sure: you will not agree with it. Oh, yes, you will agree with *some* of it; there are films included that would undoubtedly appear on everybody's list, but equally there are several, maybe many, which would not appear on any but mine. And not only will some of the inclusions upset you but so will the omissions. Why, you will wonder, was this not mentioned? Or this? Or this? Or that? And the answer quite simply is because *it is my selection* – not yours, nor anyone else's.

In any event, one of the delights – or irritations – of a book like this is the room it leaves for disagreement. When this one was first published professional critics seized upon it with glee because of the opportunity it afforded them to show how infinitely cleverer than me they were. Too much from America, they said; not enough from Europe or the Far East. 'Has this man never seen...' they said, proceeding to name numerous films that I had overlooked and their knowledgeable mention of which proved the (apparently) greater depth of their own cinemagoing experience. Of course, the fact that I hadn't included their favourites didn't mean I hadn't seen them; it just meant I hadn't included them. Still, never mind. The one who gave me the greatest pleasure was the film critic who chided me for neglecting the works of the German expressionists, then listed several examples and ended with the gloriously pompous statement: 'I must have these films about me.' Ever since I've had a recurring image of him pushing a trolley in Tesco with a video of Murnau's 1922 *Nosferatu* hanging from a string round his neck and various other bits of German expressionism sticking out of his pockets because 'I must have these films about me.' One man's list then is another man's poison, but what all lists have in common is their ability to stir up heated disagreement. In 1995 the readers of the *Sunday Times* decided in a poll that David Lean was the greatest director ever, his closest rivals being the likes of Alfred Hitchcock, Michael Curtiz, Billy Wilder, Francis Coppola, Quentin Tarantino, Martin Scorsese, Orson Welles and Stanley Kubrick. No Eisenstein, you notice, no Howard Hawks, no John Ford, no Renoir, Kurasawa, Truffaut or – dammit – Murnau but instead Quentin Tarantino who, at the time, had only made two films. Now there's the stuff of vitriolic discussion if you like. But not here; another day perhaps, in another book.

After each of the films in the present selection I have listed the leading players and the most important members of the production team. The abbreviations I have used are pretty self-explanatory but, in case there is any doubt, here is the key: DIR = director; PROD = producer; SCR = screenplay; PHOT = director of photography or cinematographer; MUS = musical composer; PROD DESIGN = production designer; ART/SET DECOR = art direction/set decoration; MUS DIR = musical director; CHOR = choreography.

The running times mentioned are the longest known to exist, although sometimes the fullest versions are difficult to find. Many films are cut for television or video release, in some cases quite drastically. Many others were originally released in the cinema at a length specified by the studio (quite often after bitter argument with the director) then later re-released at a greater length when what is known as 'the director's cut' had been restored. David Lean's *Lawrence of Arabia* is an example. (Incidentally, I attribute films to their directors not because I hold any brief for the *auteur* theory, which claims nonsensically that the director is the sole author, but because it is convenient to do so.)

So far as the Academy Awards are concerned, films are eligible for nomination in the year in which they were first released in America. With most foreign language, and some British films, this means that they crop up in the Oscar lists a year or two after they were made and released in their countries of origin. (Until 1956 foreign films were given Special Awards rather than Oscars.)

One more point: at the Cannes Film Festival a few years ago when Peter Greenaway's *The Belly of an Architect* was shown in competition I asked its star, Brian Dennehy, what he thought of it. After careful consideration he said: 'I've been in a lot of movies in my time but this is the first film I've ever made.' I know, or at least I think I know, what he meant – that a movie is something light and unsubstantial while a film is significant, a serious work with something to say. Graham Greene made a similar distinction between what he called his 'entertainments' and his serious novels.

But while I respect Dennehy's careful differentiation I haven't borrowed his definition. The purists may object but film, movie, picture, motion picture – to avoid repetition as much as anything else – I've used them all without discrimination and without giving more weight to one word than to another because in the end they all describe the same thing: a work created for the cinema.

Introduction

One – Early Days

The cinema was born on 28 December 1895, its birth pangs witnessed – though not, of course, heard since sound came much later – by a paying audience of thirty-three in a basement on the Boulevard des Capucines in Paris.

On that night in the Grand Café at the Hôtel Scribe the brothers Louis and Auguste Lumière presented a twenty-minute programme of short films featuring such momentous events as a train arriving at a station and workers leaving a factory, plus a piece of slapstick called *L'Arroseur Arrosé*, wherein a gardener is drenched by his own hosepipe. Rib-tickling stuff.

The Lumières had, in fact, shown their films several times before that year – in March for members of the Société d'Encouragement pour l'Industrie Nationale in Paris; in June for a photographers' convention in Lyons; and, the same month and back in Paris, for the Revue Générale des Sciences. But this demonstration of their work at the Hôtel Scribe was the first time, certainly in France, that the public had been invited, indeed exhorted by advertising posters, to come in and watch a movie.

Thus the Lumières came to be recognised as 'the fathers of the cinema', a most serendipitous coincidence considering that they could hardly have been more aptly named, although to bestow such a coveted title upon them is perhaps a little hard on the German, Max Sklandowsky.

On 1 November 1895 Sklandowsky and his brother, Emil, had given a public presentation of their own motion pictures at the Wintergarten in Berlin and Max, who designed the equipment, might therefore look down from wherever he is now with a sense of grievance on the plaudits heaped upon the Lumières. Given the fact that he got in nearly two months before them, was it not he – and, if you want to spread the credit, Emil – rather than they, who truly invented the cinema? There is certainly a school of thought in Germany which supports this claim, if only to put one over on the French, but the mass of cinema historians is on the side of the Lumières. The Sklandowskys' equipment, it is generally accepted, was crude stuff, not a real projector at all but a piece of appa-

3

ratus that showed a series of images rather than a continuous moving picture.

So the Lumières have it.

The parentage of moving pictures themselves, on the other hand, is much harder to pin down. In Britain and elsewhere during the 1880s, Eadweard Muybridge had been conducting important experiments in photography, which in turn strongly influenced further work by the Frenchman Étienne Jules Marey, and in America Thomas Edison, as well as contributing to the development of the telephone, the phonograph and electric light, had already, and with the assistance of William Dickson, invented a device for showing film in synchronisation with a phonograph record. (To this he gave the remarkably clumsy name of the Kinetophonograph and must have known from the start that it would never catch on.) Furthermore, let us not forget the contribution (commemorated in the 1951 film *The Magic Box*) of the Englishman William Friese-Greene who, by 1889, had already developed a primitive motion picture camera and a projection machine.

Like success, motion pictures have many fathers, none of whom could with anything approaching total justification sign his name with a flourish to the birth certificate. The Lumière brothers certainly leapt ahead of the field with the development in 1894 of the cinematographe, which combined both camera and projector, but even the French fall short of claiming that the Lumières were the inventors of motion pictures and, besides, they owed a great deal to the work of their rivals.

Nevertheless, having stolen a march on everyone else, the Lumières were quick to exploit their advantage. By 1897, while the rest of the world still looked upon movies as a curiosity, perhaps even a passing fad, to be shown in music halls and penny arcades, the brothers had opened what was in effect the first real cinema – a building in Paris designed solely for the purpose of showing films.

Even America could not claim anything like that until 1902 when a showman in Los Angeles – another happy coincidence, bearing in mind that a decade later LA was to become, or anyway start to become, the movie capital of the Western world – threw out the slot machines from his amusement arcade and put in seats and a movie projector instead.

However, by 1896 the world had film and it had cinema; what it did not have was that marriage of photography and drama which was to produce the art form of the twentieth century. But now enter a visionary, another Frenchman, Georges Méliès. Most early films simply recorded actuality; it was Méliès, a conjuror and illusionist by trade, who realised more swiftly than any of his contemporaries that while shots of a train entering a station and workers knocking off after the day shift were no doubt awfully fascinating, they did seem to lack something. A plot perhaps, character development. Even daring little numbers like Edison's *The Kiss* (1896), which showed a rather demure middle-aged couple discreetly osculating, or the eponymous *Fatima* (1897) doing her no doubt greatly admired belly dance were not, when you came right down to it, completely satisfying. You might, as people in America did, mutter, 'Good Lord, look at those filthy swine kissing. Have they no shame?' but, though outraged, you would hardly come away feeling you'd got the whole story.

What the cinema needed, Méliès decided, was a touch of fantasy; not just fact but fiction; not just actuality but illusion. So, with the use of trick photography, he made films in which a woman becomes a skeleton, female wrestlers turn into men and ghosts dance. He also mocked up fake 'newsreels' purporting to show such events of the day as a volcano erupting and the trial of Dreyfus, and quite often his audiences thought these were genuine documentaries.

With the kind of self-effacing modesty which, only too soon, was to become typical of the movers and shakers in the movie industry, Méliès was wont to declare that, in fact, he was more important to the development of the cinema than the Lumière brothers. And in one respect he had a point. If the Lumières and the other pioneers showed that it was possible to depict life and movement on film, it was Méliès who realised that with this magical new medium events could be changed, stories could be told, art could be captured and even created.

Nevertheless, it was not until around the turn of the century and the development of editing, basically the joining together of different pieces of film (and there are as many claimants to the invention of that as there are to the invention of motion pictures themselves), that narrative became a staple ingredient of the movies. A prime example of the early narrative films was Edwin Porter's *The Great Train Robbery* (1903), a one-reeler, ten minutes in duration, which tells in fourteen scenes of the robbery, the subsequent chase and the apprehension of the criminals.

Fitting in neatly with the general trend towards bragging and self-promotion that was highly popular in the film business then as later, Porter reckoned that the invention of editing was really down to him but there's no particular reason to believe him. He was, like almost everyone else in the burgeoning industry, something of a plagiarist, or at least a borrower and adaptor of other people's ideas, and even *The Great Train Robbery* was not entirely original. But what it points up is the fact that a large number of those early narrative pictures dealt with crimes and chases so that the crime movie might well be considered the very first film genre, although against that I suppose it could be said that *The Kiss* had introduced sex to the cinema even earlier.

None of this, however, is to suggest that advances in technique and content were all coming from America. In Britain, for example, an edited film called *Fire!* was made as early as 1901; in France in 1904 Méliès made probably the world's first two-reeler, *Voyage à Travers l'Impossible*; while Sarah Bernhardt starred as *Queen Elizabeth* in a four-reeler in 1912. And if that seemed long – and by all accounts it did – *Quo Vadis?*, directed in Italy by Enrico Guazzoni also in 1912, ran to twice the length and confounded the sceptics, who insisted that audiences could not sit through more than a few minutes of flickering film, by becoming a big popular success in America. Two years later, again from Italy, came Giovanni Pastrone's three-hour *Cabiria*.

What this meant was that already, less than twenty years after that evening in the Boulevard des Capucines, motion pictures were offering themselves as a full-blown entertainment medium. An evening at the cinema – or, in America, the nickelodeon, a nickel being the price of admission – was now an acceptable alternative to an evening at the theatre, especially as movies were beginning to last as long as plays. All right, there was no sound – except the piano accompaniment – but what did you want for a nickel?

Now at this stage and up to the First World War no single country dominated the film industry. Developments were happening as fast in Europe as in America and it was, comparatively, a free market. The films were silent, so there was no language barrier, and most countries produced films as well as importing and exporting them. Even Denmark, though specialising to some extent in sex movies – *The White Slave Trade* in 1910, for instance – was a significant source of what would now be known as 'product'. I say 'even Denmark' not because I wish to patronise the Danes, but because if you think of Denmark today, you don't necessarily think of movies – bacon, butter and cheese perhaps but not movies.

What's more there was no star system. The actors in films, unless they happened to be Sarah Bernhardt, were unidentified and in many cases weren't even actors at all but merely friends and relatives of the film makers who had been drafted in to go through the motions. In those early days the nearest approximation the cinema had, even in America, to what we would now call movie stars were 'the Biograph Girl' and 'the Girl with the Curls'. The former, later filched from the Biograph company by Carl Laemmle to work for his own Independent Motion Pictures, was the euphoniously named Florence Lawrence and the latter turned out to be Mary Pickford.

Lawrence, whose career was otherwise undistinguished and petered out in the 1920s, had the distinction of being the first film performer whose name was known to the public. Her frequent appearance in Biograph's films had meant that her face was familiar and much admired but nobody knew who she was until Laemmle lured her away and, pulling off what is surely the first major publicity stunt in movie history, finally revealed her identity.

In order to make sure that the cinema-going audience would know that the Biograph Girl was no longer the Biograph Girl but had been transmuted instead into the IMP Girl, he planted a story in the press to the effect that poor Florence Lawrence was no more, that she had been killed in a streetcar accident. Then, with the public still no doubt reeling from its shock and grief, he planted another story claiming that the earlier report had been a fabrication by his enemies and that Miss Lawrence was happily alive and well, and, by sheer chance, happened to be working for him.

That piece of monumental hype was, in effect, the beginning of the star system. The knowledge that Lawrence and, incidentally, the Girl with the Curls, who had been wooed away from Biograph at much the same time, were now contracted to IMP gave Laemmle's productions extra clout at the box office, a fact not lost on his rivals. Within three years most companies were advertising the names of their leading players, although they and their successors later had cause to regret the fact. While anonymous actors could be picked up, or even dragged in off the street, for a few dollars a day, established names came much more expensive. When Florence Lawrence left Biograph for IMP her salary was raised from $25 to $1,000 a week. The floodgates were open and the day of the million-dollar movie star was not far off.

Two – The Golden Age

One day in Buenos Aires a group of us, who courtesy of Cubby Broccoli and United Artists had been watching Roger Moore doing his stuff as *007* in a couple of scenes from *Moonraker*, were discussing the difference between European and American television. We decided without much difficulty, since we were all Europeans, that our television was, of course, much better than their television. But why?

An academic who was also a film critic on TV in Denmark proffered this suggestion: in Europe television was introduced and, certainly at first, controlled by intellectuals; in America it was both introduced and controlled from the start by advertising men. Thus in Europe it was seen, during its infancy anyway, as a medium to inform and entertain, while in America it was seized upon as a medium to help sell things.

There is, I feel, a certain grain of truth in this, or at least there was. These days, with the introduction of commercial channels in most countries and, particularly in Britain with the advent of satellite TV, everyone else is moving closer to the American way of thinking. Mass audiences attract advertisers and the lowest common denominator attracts mass audiences. In Britain the BBC, which – at present anyway – does not carry commercials, should be immune to this pernicious scrabble for ratings but, thanks to government pressure (especially in the 1980s), it is not. To justify its existence and more specifically the licence fee it needs to attract a healthy percentage of the available viewers. Thus the American view seems to have prevailed: TV is for selling things, if only (as in the case of the BBC) the service itself.

And as with TV so, broadly speaking, with the movies. I don't mean that the early pioneers in America were any less intellectual than their European counterparts or that they saw the cinema merely as a fast way to make a buck. Men like D.W. Griffith, director of *Birth of a Nation*, were quick to realise the artistic possibilities of this wondrous new toy, but equally there were entrepreneurs no less swift to comprehend the amazing opportunities it offered to make money.

This was a medium that might gave been made to measure for America, a vast country which, at the turn of the century, had a large immigrant population many of whom could barely speak English. These people would have had little use for the theatre, even assuming they lived within striking distance of one, or for most of the books they could buy because they had insufficient grasp of the language. But the movies – the silent movies – these they could all understand, so what America had more than any European country was a huge captive audience, a large proportion of them pretty well uneducated. And what these people wanted were simple stories in which, never mind the fact that the captions might be incomprehensible, the action told all.

In feeding the growing demand for screen entertainment America was, of course, greatly helped by the First World War, a fixture which the United States sat out until 1917 before, as it were, coming on to the pitch as a late but highly effective substitute. Between 1914 and 1918 the making of films was not exactly high on the list of any European country's priorities. Pictures continued to be made but not to the same extent as before, and to cover the shortfall in foreign imports America had to increase its own production. By the end of the decade, with Hollywood, rather than New York, now firmly established as the centre of the industry, America was well on its way to monopolising the world market.

Of what, in the golden age of American movies, became the nine major studios, the first to establish itself in Hollywood was Paramount in its earlier incarnation as the Jesse Lasky Feature Play Company. Lasky formed this outfit in 1913 with his lawyer, his brother-in-law Samuel Goldfish – who later, and doubtless feeling that Goldfish lacked the ring of authority, changed his name to Goldwyn – and an actor of no great ability called Cecil B. de Mille. Their first production was a western, *The Squaw Man*, which, though it was actually set in Wyoming, they decided to film at Flagstaff, Arizona. But when de Mille, now turned director, arrived in Flagstaff he didn't like the place at all; the weather was lousy for a start. So he got back on the train and finally alighted in Hollywood, a suburb of Los Angeles that consisted mostly of orange groves and sunshine. De Mille was not particularly interested in the oranges but he was greatly in favour of the sunshine, so he promptly hired a large barn and settled down to make his movie.

Films had been made in Hollywood before but de Mille's barn was very possibly the first studio to be established there, though the first purpose-built studio was opened by Universal in 1915. Others soon followed – United Artists, Warner Brothers, Columbia, MGM and RKO by the end of the 1920s and 20th Century Fox a few years later. I suppose they would all have fetched up there eventually but it's at least mildly interesting to speculate on what might have happened if it hadn't been raining in Flagstaff the day de Mille turned up. Would he have rented a barn there? And if he had, would the other companies have decided that Flagstaff was the place to be? Would the words 'a typical Flagstaff movie' now trip off the tongue as lightly as 'a typical Hollywood movie' do? Somehow I doubt it. Flagstaff is too guttural; Hollywood has a softer, more agreeable sound. Mind you, though I have no idea what Flagstaff is like today, I would not be surprised if any of its residents, seeing the ramshackle, sometimes sleazy urban sprawl that Hollywood has become, felt grateful that de Mille decided to move on.

The film industry did Hollywood no favours. It brought employment and to some people – most of them newcomers rather than the indigenous population – great wealth, but it turned a peaceful rural area into a factory town. Now even the factories are not what they were, the acres of land which used to comprise the back lots around the major studios having been sold off for industrial and commercial development since the 1950s when television replaced the cinema as the world's biggest medium for mass entertainment and the movie companies found themselves strapped for cash.

Clark Gable's advice to aspiring stars arriving in Hollywood in the 1930s was:'Never buy anything you can't put on the Chief' – the Chief being the train back to the East Coast – and that air of impermanence still exists. Architecturally the place is a mess, the buildings along Sunset Boulevard a jumble of mostly undistinguished constructions which look as if they could easily be torn down and replaced overnight without anybody really noticing. Only when, going westwards, you reach the affluence of Beverly Hills is there any sign that people are actually living here rather than simply being in a state of transit, of passing through, of hanging around only until it's time to catch the Chief (or its modern-day jumbo jet equivalent) and return to a *real* city, such as Chicago or New York.

Sunset Boulevard, which I always think is the most magically and evocatively named street in the world, is pleasant enough from the moment it hits Beverly Hills and starts winding its way to the Pacific Coast Highway, although to appreciate it a lot you would have to love suburbia, especially very, very rich suburbia. You would have to admire large, beautifully kept houses – or in many cases bungalows – in equally well-tended though sometimes unsuitably small plots, which surround them like a too-tight collar, where the only sign of human life is an occasional Mexican gardener pruning something. But eastwards from the Beverly Hills boundary, up through Sunset Strip and beyond, it is disappointingly, shockingly tacky, an expanse of hotels, motels, liquor stores and fast-food joints that seems to stretch endlessly, pointlessly, into the distance. To reach any kind of centre at all you have to turn left and find the intersection of Hollywood Boulevard and Highland. Mann's (formerly Grauman's) Chinese Theatre is there, a little way back from the road, its small forecourt studded with the palm and footprints of the stars, the sidewalk leading to and away from it bearing the names of other, lesser, stars. But this, too, is a tatty shrine to the immortals of the screen. Tourist guides and shops and stalls peddling overpriced and worthless souvenirs to the out-of-town visitors ply their trade all around. Hollywood movies at their best have style, grace and elegance; Hollywood itself has none of these qualities. Unless you have business there it is a place to drive into, pause awhile to look round and then, as swiftly as possible, drive out of again.

The romantic view of Hollywood and its environs in the early days – before television and the pop music industry moved in to spoil everything – was of a village, a small community of beautiful, famous men and women, all of whom knew each other and entertained each other lavishly at wild and extravagant parties. But that was never really true. No doubt the parties took place but there was no village-type community or anything like it. Joseph L. Mankiewicz, writer, director and multiple Oscar winner, once told me that even in its heyday Hollywood consisted in fact of a series of minor baronies, each jealous of its own territory. If, for instance, you worked at MGM, yes, you knew everyone at MGM but you didn't know anyone at Warner Brothers or Columbia or Fox or Paramount, nor were you encouraged to know them. To mix with people from other studios was to arouse the suspicion that you were thinking of leaving and that cast doubt on your corporate loyalty.

As an example of how little like a village Hollywood was, consider the following: two of its greatest stars, Henry Fonda and Katharine Hepburn, had been in pictures since, respectively, 1935 and 1932, but they were never even introduced to each other until they started filming *On Golden Pond* in 1981. Fonda was then 76 and Hepburn 74; they hadn't met before because they had always worked at different studios.

Hollywood is not so much a place as a state of mind. Or rather, it's more attractive as a state of mind than it is as a place. Flagstaff should think itself lucky.

If by the beginning of the 1920s America was the world leader in film production, it was not then – nor has it been since – pre-eminent in developing film as an art form. Hollywood is not interested in art; it is interested in money and the two rarely go together. To Hollywood, film is, and virtually always has been, an industry. There is, I submit, nothing contemptible in this attitude. The manufacturer of decent, serviceable and mass-produced furniture is not to be despised because he isn't Chippendale. You might wish he were but that's another matter. So Hollywood swiftly recognised film and the cinema as an *entertainment* medium with a unique ability both to put bums on seats and money in the pockets of producers, distributors and exhibitors and, by and large, left it to others to develop its potentialities as a means of creating art.

So while by 1920 or thereabouts Hollywood may have had in Charlie Chaplin a supreme creative artist, it valued him more as a bankable star whose name (as John Lennon later claimed for The Beatles) was probably better known worldwide than that of Jesus Christ. Generally speaking, the efforts to extend the boundaries of film – to show that it could encompass more than simple chases, romances and slapstick – were being made elsewhere. In Germany, for instance, the political and social confusion of the immediate postwar period led to expressionism, *The Cabinet of Dr Caligari* in 1919 being perhaps the first significant example. *The Oxford Companion to Film* describes expressionism as 'a movement in the graphic arts, literature, drama and film which flourished in Germany 1903–1933. Its main aim was the externalisation of man's inner world, particularly the elemental emotions of fear, hatred, love and anxiety.' These days, most serious – and sometimes not so serious – films attempt to do something like that as a matter of course, albeit in a less stark, more subtle way than the early Germans; in the 1920s it was a revelation.

In Britain, however, production had become virtually moribund since the First World War. By the mid-1920s probably ninety per cent of the films seen in Britain were American and matters only began to improve in 1927 when the Cinematograph (or Quota) Act decreed that henceforth five per cent – rising over a decade to twenty per cent – of films shown in cinemas must be of British origin. But for the most part this simply meant more, not better, production. The French industry, too, took a long while to recover from the war but there at least a brief flowering of the impressionist and surrealist schools of film-making, plus the work of directors like Abel Gance, showed a conviction that film was to be taken quite as seriously as music, literature or the theatre.

Meanwhile Russian film makers, especially Sergei Eisenstein with *Strike* and *The Battleship Potemkin*, were developing advanced techniques in editing and montage – the use of sequences to convey background information, ideas and intellectual rather than emotional points. Montage is the stone lions rearing up in *Potemkin* or Chaplin seeing commuters as a flock of sheep in *Modern Times*. Hollywood was not slow to learn from its foreign competitors or to assimilate and adapt their ideas, but with regard to the style and content of film-making it was and still is far more in the business of learning than of teaching.

It's in technical development that America leads the way. It was America, after all, that revolutionised the entire industry in 1927 when Warner Brothers launched talking pictures with *The Jazz Singer*. Never mind that experiments in sound had been going on for decades in Europe as well; it was America that took the plunge and thereby tightened its grip on the industry, certainly in the West. By 1930 the silent movie had practically disappeared in the USA and Western Europe – in Britain in 1929, for example, Hitchcock started filming *Blackmail* as a silent but then turned it into a talkie – and countries such as Japan and Russia followed suit a few years later. But this traumatic change naturally led to confusion.

Hitherto film had been an international medium; mime spoke for itself; simple captions in one language could easily be replaced by equally simple captions in another. A silent film from Germany, France or Italy was immediately accessible in any other country. Nevertheless, the main target for foreign exporters was the vast USA market because, although Russia, too, had a huge captive audience it was mostly for its own productions.

But when film found its voice it tended to speak increasingly in American accents and that, of course, caused difficulties. Foreign films were now recognisably foreign and incomprehensible to most Americans. Subtitles would have provided no real solution: they have never been popular because audiences would rather listen than read. Dubbing was one answer but it worked better for Hollywood, where many of the early talkies were made simultaneously in two or three languages, than for anyone else. Besides, the major studios rapidly set up distribution offices throughout the world; other nations were neither as swift nor as effective in doing the same thing in the USA. So the market for movies in anything but English (and even then preferably in American English) began to shrink. And this was where the business acumen of the Hollywood moguls, together with their willingness to buy, borrow or steal ideas and talent from other countries, began to tell.

The production side of the American industry was run by people like Sam Goldwyn, who had started out as a glove salesman; Harry Cohn, Head of Columbia, a former song plugger in the music industry; and Louis Mayer, of MGM, a one-time scrap dealer. These men were not intellectuals but they weren't fools either, not by a long way. What they were was businessmen, people who understood the laws of supply and demand, of profit and loss, of giving the customer what he wanted. If the cinema could produce art, fine, they had no objection and they were certainly astute enough to recognise and even appreciate it if it were served up to them on a platter. But their main concern was to make money for their stockholders; the way to do that was by giving the public what it liked best and by and large the public was only interested in cinematic art if it contained some combination of laughter, tears, adventure and excitement. On the whole art did not make money.

But at the same time the movie moguls were eager to hire artists from aboard and teach them to apply their talents to popular entertainment. So from Hungary came the likes of Bela Lugosi, Alexander Korda and the director Michael Curtiz; Sweden provided Greta Garbo; from Germany and Austria came Ernst Lubitsch, Billy Wilder, Otto Preminger, Marlene Dietrich, Erich von Stroheim, Josef von Sternberg, Robert Siodmak, William Wyler and many more; Britain provided a healthy stream of actors and directors, from Ronald Colman to Leslie Howard and Basil Rathbone, from James Whale to Alfred Hitchcock.

If America was an international melting pot, then Hollywood was America in miniature and all these exotic imports played their part in shaping Hollywood films. It was the Armenian-born Rouben Mamoulian, for instance, who in *Applause* in 1929 brought in twin soundtracks and devised a way of moving the enormously heavy new sound cameras to and fro to restore fluidity to tracking shots. Two years later in *City Streets* he also introduced the concept of subjective sound to feature films – Sylvia Sidney sitting up in bed and hearing Gary Cooper's voice in her thoughts.

The American industry had the organisation, the flair and, despite the

Wall Street crash, the money to experiment, to be innovative. One classic film genre, the western, was entirely American and another, the musical, originated there. After all, *The Jazz Singer* could claim to be the first musical as well as the first talkie since Al Jolson sang half a dozen songs in it.

In the development of colour, too, Hollywood was the leader. Some kind of colour, usually tinting, had been used in many silent films from around 1910 onwards, and as early as 1923 de Mille experimented with an early form of Technicolor for some scenes in *The Ten Commandments*. But the first movie to be made entirely in three-strip Technicolor was *Becky Sharp*, again directed by Rouben Mamoulian, in 1935.

The 1930s represented the golden age of the American film industry. This was the time when the Hollywood studios were totally in control – of the actors, the writers, the directors, the producers; the time when films were devised with specific stars in mind, Gable, Tracy, Cagney, Cooper, Garbo, Davis, Crawford, Shearer, Stanwyck and many more; the time when, as Joe Mankiewicz told me, there was not a novel published nor a play staged almost anywhere in the world that was not brought to the attention of the studio moguls. They did not actually read or watch all these things, of course they didn't; they were busy men. (Jack Warner, having bought the screen rights to *Antony Adverse*, was asked if he had read it yet. 'Read it?' he said, 'I can't even lift it.') But they were aware of everything that was going on. They read synopses of synopses of every book or play that might, just possibly, be worth turning into a movie.

By now Hollywood was firmly established as the mecca for international talent and this was reflected in the quality of the films made there. Power, affluence and command of most of the world market created a confidence which, in turn, led to the production of films of such skill, elegance, style and wit as no other national cinema has ever been able to approach. Individual film makers from many parts of the world have equalled and often surpassed Hollywood's best; but no other country has ever had an industry whose overall output could begin to compare.

In truth, though, there was little competition in the 1930s. Japanese and Russian films were rarely seen outside their own lands. Germany, having driven out most of its creative people, was increasingly absorbed in making political propaganda movies. So, too, was Italy. Even the introduction there in 1932 of the world's first international film festival at Venice was marred, to say the least, by the swift realisation that only films of Fascist inclination stood much chance of winning. It was indignation at this state of affairs that induced the French to set up a rival festival at Cannes in 1939, although, in the event, the intervening global unpleasantness caused its debut to be postponed until 1946. France, however, was one country whose film industry flourished as brightly – although not with the same international impact – as America's during the 1930s. Directors like Marcel Carné, Jean Renoir and René Clair were turning out work of such quality as to provide, as it were, an *haute cuisine* alternative to America's basic meat and potatoes.

Britain, meanwhile, was doing its best to ape Hollywood – even to the establishment of a studio called Pinewood – and suffering in the process. For the most part the films that were made to fill the quota were notable for little more than that, although producers like Alexander Korda and Michael Balcon were doing their best to raise the standard, while John Grierson made a highly significant contribution by founding the British documentary movement. The 1930s were by no means totally barren from the British point of view. Films such as Korda's *The Private Life of Henry VIII* and Anthony Asquith's *Pygmalion* (which won an Oscar for George Bernard Shaw of all unlikely people) were very successful and Alfred Hitchcock made two of his best pictures, *The Thirty-Nine Steps* and *The Lady Vanishes*. But by 1939 even Hitchcock had succumbed to the richer rewards that America offered, for Hollywood's motto seemed to be: 'If you can't beat them, buy them', and it worked. But then it usually does.

The golden age shone most brightly at the end of the decade. The ten films nominated for best picture (yes, there were ten, not five, movies nominated in those days) in the 1939 Academy Awards included *Gone with the Wind, Goodbye Mr Chips, Mr Smith Goes to Washington, Ninotchka, Of Mice and Men, Stagecoach, The Wizard of Oz* and *Wuthering Heights*, every one of which has since found its way into some list or other of classical movies.

The advent of war (for Europe in 1939, for America in 1941) inevitably brought massive changes. Under Nazi occupation the French cinema, lacking the likes of René Clair and Jean Renoir who had gone to Hollywood, more or less stood still. Every script had to be vetted and approved by the German or Vichy censors, so it was hardly surprising that although production actually increased in the early years of the war, the films had only the most tenuous contact with reality, the output concentrating heavily on thrillers and fantasy. Marcel Carné, for instance, made an innocuous, though beautiful, medieval fairy tale, *Les Visiteurs du Soir*, in 1942. The Devil appears in this and though he could be equated with Hitler you'd have to strain hard to spot the connection. Similarly when Robert Bresson, later to become one of France's most influential directors, made his debut as such in 1943 it was with *Les Anges du Péché*, set safely and uncontroversially in a convent.

Meanwhile the German cinema, now totally in the hands of the propaganda minister, Joseph Goebbels, was little less than disgusting. The use in that country of film to disseminate political ideals was seen early and clearly in Leni Riefenstahl's brilliant but worrying documentary, *Triumph of the Will*, which in 1935 propagated the notion of Deutschland über Alles. But this was mild, unobjectionable stuff compared with the vicious – even, when looked at now, demented – anti-Semitic propaganda that was to come later. Films like Veit Harlan's *Jew Süss* and Franz Hippler's *The Eternal Jew*, both made in 1939, have won places in infamy. These, and many others almost as bad but possibly less effective because they were even cruder, depicted the Jew, grotesquely caricatured, as the world's enemy, the antichrist. That they flourished is no doubt attributable to a variety of reasons: British and American movies, were, of course, banned; the German people were apparently brainwashed by Hitler; and no German film from 1936 onwards ever had a bad review, because Goebbels had thoughtfully forbidden all criticism on the grounds that the reporting of art had nothing to do with quality or aesthetic values but should be confined to mere description.

The use of film as propaganda, however, was by no means unique to Germany. In Britain the national delight in using comedy, satire or just general mickey-taking to diminish the enemy was exploited by Will Hay in, for example, *The Goose Steps Out* in 1942. Other popular comedians of the time, such as Arthur Askey, Tommy Trinder and George Formby, also starred in movies designed either to poke fun at the ludicrous Nazis or at least to keep the national morale in good order. Thrillers, too, were tailored to help the war effort: Leslie Howard starring in *Pimpernel Smith* (1941) as a British agent rescuing imprisoned scientists from the blockheaded Huns, and in the same year with Laurence Olivier in *The 49th Parallel*, wherein a fanatical Nazi U-boat crew led by Eric Portman is outwitted and destroyed in Canada.

And so it went on with films like Noël Coward's *In Which We Serve*,

Anthony Asquith's *We Dive at Dawn* and Carol Reed's *The Way Ahead* extolling British heroism and resilience and at least suggesting the inevitability of ultimate Allied victory.

But the greatest and most subtle of all wartime propaganda movies was *Casablanca* with its pre-Pearl Harbor message to America to wake up and take a close look at what was going on in Europe. In the years leading up to the war the Hollywood studios (with the honourable exception of Warner Brothers, which had shut down its Berlin Office after its Jewish representative there had been kicked to death by Nazis in 1936) were reluctant to upset Hitler because Germany was a lucrative market. But certainly from 1940 onwards they gave full support to their future allies. Tyrone Power and Robert Taylor were American volunteers in the British forces in, respectively, *A Yank in the RAF* and *Flight Command*; Errol Flynn, who, with his Anglo-Australian background, could be a Yank or not depending on your point of view, starred in *Dive Bomber*; and, not least, there was Greer Garson as the immortal *Mrs Miniver*. After Pearl Harbor, of course, America could and did make propaganda movies about its own armed forces at war and also, like Britain, used comedy to boost morale. Lubitsch's glorious *To Be or Not To Be* is, in effect, a hilarious piece of anti-Nazi propaganda.

Hollywood indeed thrived during the war years. The demand for entertainment was possibly keener than ever and though some of the best directors, John Ford, Frank Capra and William Wyler among them, were much involved in making documentaries to aid the war effort, there were plenty of others left to provide the escapism that the public wanted. More significantly it was around 1944 and 1945 that *film noir*, a genre or anyway a concept that still excites movie makers today, was not exactly invented but certainly established. The basis of *film noir* is, of course, darkness, not simply a darkness of look but a darkness of content, of spirit; nothing is quite what it seems, nobody – least of all a woman – is to be trusted; the hero is tough, cynical, fatalistic; in *film noir*, no matter how the story finishes up, there are no real happy endings. With hindsight many people now see John Huston's 1941 thriller, *The Maltese Falcon*, as the first film in the genre, though it came to full flower a few years later with movies such as Edward Dmytryk's *Murder My Sweet*, Billy Wilder's *Double Indemnity*, Fritz Lang's *The Woman in the Window* and Otto Preminger's *Laura*. To some extent this kind of film, redolent of doubt and anxiety, reflected the concerns of a nation which, seeing victory approaching, now began to worry about the problems that peacetime would pose. There was anxiety about employment for the returning troops, about whether women, who had come out of the home to play a vital role in keeping industry at full throttle, would happily return to the kitchen now their menfolks were back. Women had gained power and freedom during the war and men resented and feared that. But if this helps to account for the mood, though never the content, of the genre, it doesn't altogether account for the look. And that, in fact, owed a great deal to economy. America, unlike Europe, suffered few shortages during the war, but film still had to be used sparingly; there was pressure on directors to complete their pictures as fast as possible. Dmytryk, for example, said that he used what was known as 'broad brush lighting' – lighting the figure in the foreground and letting shadows fall across everything else – because it was cheaper and quicker; there was no time for anything more elaborate. French film critics, who, after the war, invented the name *film noir*, thought that what Dmytryk and the others had done to change the look and mood of pictures was a stroke of pure invention. To an extent perhaps it was, but that is to overlook the maternity of invention, which, as we all know, is necessity.

Nevertheless, with this kind of exciting innovation and the increased appetite for screen entertainment during and immediately after the Second World War, Hollywood's golden age continued – its lustre, to be sure, dimming gradually – throughout the 1940s. But then the filament broke and the light went out completely in the mid-1950s when television robbed the cinema of its audiences and destroyed the power of the studios.

Three – Babies, Telly and Other Disasters

Many factors have been blamed for the decline of the cinema after the Second World War and, no doubt, each made its contribution. In America – always, in the movie industry, a useful yardstick by which to measure what goes on elsewhere – they pointed to increased postwar affluence, which provided people with a wider choice of leisure-time activities, and to a remarkable baby boom, the result presumably of generously enthusiastic welcomes to home-coming troops. The latter indeed may well help to account for the fact that while cinema attendances were encouragingly high in 1946, they began to fall sharply the following year. Since it was widely accepted that women, rather than their menfolks, were the ringleaders in organising trips to the movies it was perhaps to be expected that with an unusual number of them either too heavily pregnant or too recently delivered of offspring to move about much the box-office take would suffer.

But the most powerful enemy was, of course, television. For three decades the cinema had been the greatest medium for mass entertainment the world had ever known or, quite possibly, could ever imagine, its only significant rival in that time being radio, which in the 1930s and 40s was a great deal more popular than is perhaps realised today. Television – radio with pictures delivered at negligible cost into your own living-room – was an adversary against which even the film industry could not successfully compete. As more and more homes acquired a telly, so more and more cinemas felt the draught and the once omnipotent studios were obliged to cut their costs.

The whole studio system, which for so long had kept creative talent on exclusive contract and therefore in thrall to the Hollywood moguls and the New York money men, fell apart. Nobody, not even MGM, the mightiest of them all, could now afford to carry scores of actors, directors, producers and writers on a weekly payroll. So the stars went freelance and discovered that, by demanding a fee for their services plus a percentage of the box-office gross, they were a lot better off. Or anyway the big ones were. Gradually, as their influence diminished, the role of the studios had less to do with actually making films than with backing and distributing independent productions.

(Though perhaps for different reasons, much the same thing is happening today in British television. As a result of the new franchises bought and sold in 1991, the old-style programme-making companies, such as Thames, have gone out of fashion to be replaced by consortia which themselves create little, but mostly buy product from independent outfits.)

But this is not to say that the Hollywood studios threw up their hands and wimpishly surrendered to their rival. To win back the vanishing audience they tried all manner of desperate capers. TV in those early days was exclusively black and white, so now films were nearly always made in colour. TV sets were very small, so the cinema screen grew bigger. There was Cinemascope, there was 70mm, there was Cinerama, there was 3-D. TV was intimate, largely a matter of close-ups and two-shots, so films became ever more expensive as the studios poured their hopes and their money into musicals, epics and all-action spectaculars. De Mille remade *The Ten Commandments*, William Wyler directed the multiple Oscar winner *Ben-Hur*, Joseph L. Mankiewicz's *Cleopatra* was so expensive that it nearly ruined 20th Century Fox; there were lavish musicals such as *Annie Get Your Gun, Oklahoma, Kiss Me Kate* and *Singin' in the Rain*; 3-D figured in *House of Wax*; Mike Todd launched the hugely ambitious *Around the World in 80 Days*, and so it went.

Some of these measures worked for some of the time but the fact remained that TV had not only moved the goal posts but rewritten the rules of the game. Once even ordinary movies were virtually sure to make a profit but not any more; people could get ordinary at home, much of the early television being little better than the old B pictures. Now when folks took the trouble to go out in search of entertainment they wanted something different, something indeed extraordinary. Thus the content, not merely the style, of films had to change. The cinema could no longer command the masses; it had to appeal instead to a minority audience – a very large minority, certainly, but a minority for all that, and what's more a choosey one.

Ironically in Europe, where television was slower to catch on anyway, change was already happening. In Italy the neorealism school, inspired to some extent by Luchino Visconti's *Ossessione* in 1942, had been carried on and developed by the likes of Roberto Rossellini with *Rome, Open City* and Vittorio de Sica with *Bicycle Thieves*. They, and other directors, had deliberately moved away from the confines of a studio and taken their cameras into the streets to add actuality and immediacy to their stories. In many cases, too, they used 'real' people as opposed to professional actors, who, except in rare cases, should never be confused with 'real' people. Most of us have in our heads a fantasy world in which we would like to live but know that we never can; actors, on the other hand, become actors because they have plunged wholeheartedly into this fantasy world and spend their lives trying to make it come true. Thus the use of non professionals playing, in effect, themselves (as in *Bicycle Thieves*) lends a film an air of naturalism that trained actors could never create. In that respect neorealism could almost be regarded as a throwback to the kind of cod documentaries that Georges Méliès was making at the end of the nineteenth century.

In France, meanwhile, during this time of upheaval the sternly intellectual young critics of that influential magazine, *Cahiers du Cinema* – among them Jean-Luc Godard, Claude Chabrol and François Truffaut – were expounding the theory of the *auteur* and were about to introduce the *nouvelle vague* by turning movie directors themselves. The *auteur* theory is based on the not really tenable notion that the true and only author of a film is the director. In some cases – Godard, Truffaut, Ingmar Bergman, Federico Fellini are just a few examples – when the director also writes the screenplay and maybe acts as producer, this might be grudgingly conceded or at least part-conceded. But on the whole I find the concept of the *auteur* highly suspect since so many other influences are brought to bear on the making of a film. What about the contributions of the actors, of the cinematographer, of the editor, of the music composer? All these people might well be influenced by the director, but to deny that they could have made any significant individual contribution to the whole strikes me as extremely wrong-headed, not to say arrogant.

Nevertheless the *auteur* theory, suspect though it might be, added a considerable amount of fun to life and, certainly in France, led to the added lionisation of outstanding directors such as John Ford, Alfred Hitchcock and Howard Hawks, as well as conferring possibly undeserved honour on able journeymen like Samuel Fuller, Don Siegel and Budd Boetticher. Siegel may perhaps have later earned the distinction so liberally granted to him by the *Cahiers* critics with films like *Dirty Harry* and *Charlie Varrick*, but most of the others were, and remained, B-movie makers.

However, the young men of *Cahiers* had the courage and self-confidence to put their ideas into practice by becoming directors themselves, eschewing the old notions of the 'well-made' film in favour of the personal (i.e. the director's) style. That they were able to do so was partly due to the fact that the French cinema was rather desperate at the time (the late 1950s) for low-budget movies and also to the fact that private investment money became available. Success was immediate. At the Cannes Film Festival in 1959 Truffaut's *Les Quatre-Cent Coups* won the prize for best direction and Alain Resnais's *Hiroshima Mon Amour* the International Critics' Prize. In that year, twenty-four directors had made their first feature films in France and they were followed in 1960 by forty-three more debutants. Though few of these people were ever heard from again, the *nouvelle vague* had been most comprehensively launched and the great commercial success of, for example, Godard's *A Bout de Souffle* ensured that it would stay afloat.

The *auteur* concept was, not surprisingly, seized upon with delight in Hollywood – where rampant egotism is not entirely unknown – and in isolated pockets it still flourishes there, though it has been widely discredited elsewhere.

This turbulent period of change and transition also saw the international emergence of the Japanese cinema. In 1951 Akira Kurosawa's *Rashomon* won the Grand Prix at the Venice festival and made European and American audiences aware, as they had never been before, of the power and individuality of Japanese films. In the West Kurosawa himself was at once recognised as a master, though his fellow countrymen have been slow to confer this title upon him. 'In Japan,' he once told me, 'I'm regarded simply as a commercial film maker' – and this even after the enormous worldwide success (both commercial and critical) of such films as *The Seven Samurai, Kagemusha* and *Ran*. The last time I met him was at Cannes in 1990 when his film *Dreams* had been chosen to open the festival. Then I reminded him of what he had told me before and, bearing in mind that by now he had become virtually canonised by the likes of Steven Spielberg, Martin Scorsese and Frances Coppola, asked if attitudes had changed back in Japan. 'No,' he said 'When I go home after this I will once again be a beggar, humbly asking for money to make my next picture.'

That I was not entirely astonished by this admission is perhaps due to the fact that I live in Britain, where film makers are equally disregarded. In 1980 I had a drink with Alan Parker in New York, where he was directing *Fame*, and asked him when, if ever, he would make another film in Britain.

'The next one,' he said. 'I promise you. I'm coming home to make the next one.' Six months later I met him again at a private preview of *Fame* in London. 'So tell me, Alan,' I said, 'whereabouts in Britain are you making your next picture?'

He shuffled a bit, shamefacedly, and said, 'Well, actually I'm doing it in America.' I gave him my most knowing and cynical smirk and he said, 'No, honestly, it's not like you think. I wanted to work here, really I did, but I couldn't even get arrested in this country. I went to everyone you could think of trying to set up a picture and nobody was interested. You've no idea how depressing it was.' As it transpired his next film, *Shoot the Moon* with Albert Finney and Diane Keaton, was indeed made in America with American money and Parker has not made a feature film in Britain since. Indeed, he has not made a feature film in Britain since *Bugsy Malone* in 1976; the nearest he has come in the interim is Dublin where he filmed *The Commitments*.

I mention this because it merely exemplifies the distressing myopia of the British film industry since the Second World War. Until the advent of Independent Television in 1955, giving the public the choice of two channels instead of one, the British cinema was still doing pretty well, suffering inevitably from the competition of home entertainment but nevertheless bearing up. Rank was turning out a regular programme of films from Pinewood, as was Associated British from Elstree, and at Ealing Studios the indigenous industry had achieved the richest flowering it has ever known. From there in the 1950s came all the memorable comedies – from *Whisky Galore* to *Kind Hearts and Coronets*, from *The Lavender Hill Mob* to *The Man in the White Suit* – as well as war stories such as *The Cruel Sea* and *Dunkirk* and social drama like *Mandy* and *The Shiralee*, which Peter Finch described as his favourite among all his films. But by 1960 even Ealing had gone out of business, the famous studios having been sold to the BBC.

During the 1960s, however, the British industry was protected from the worst ravages of the early television age by the injection of American money. Because it was cheaper to film in Europe than in the United States, what were known in Hollywood as 'runaway productions' became common both on the Continent and in the UK. For instance, William Wyler's *Ben-Hur* (of which the American satirist Mort Sahl said, 'Loved Ben, hated Hur') was made in Rome, as was John Huston's

The Bible; Anthony Mann filmed *El Cid* on location in Spain; *Casino Royale* (in which David Niven played James Bond) was shot in Paris; even John Wayne turned up in Madrid to co-star with Claudia Cardinale in *Circus World*. These and many others were all American films, made with American money for American studios.

But it was in Britain that the US influence during the 1960s was seen at its greatest. During that decade, as Alexander Walker points out in his book *Hollywood, England*, nearly ninety per cent of the finance for films made in Britain came from America. At the time people in this country talked of the renaissance of the British industry, and indeed there was a great deal of exciting local talent about, but to focus on the talent alone and ignore the financial source which gave it the chance to develop was dangerously short-sighted. So-called British movies made a tremendous impact during the 60s but when the decade ended and the Americans and their money went home it became clear that, from the vitally important financial aspect, these had not really been British films at all but American films, and there was no native industry worth speaking of.

Mind you, in the interim a great deal of British talent had emerged. Films like *Look Back in Anger, The Entertainer, Saturday Night and Sunday Morning, The Loneliness of the Long Distance Runner, Tom Jones* (winner of four Oscars and six other nominations in 1963), *Darling, Alfie, The Ipcress File* and *Oliver!* gave international prominence to actors like Albert Finney, Tom Courtney, Michael Caine and Julie Christie and to such directors as Tony Richardson, Karel Reisz, Lewis Gilbert and John Schlesinger. A number of these pictures were made under the banner of Woodfall, the company formed by Richardson and the playwright John Osborne. But in almost every case they, and many other successful British films of the 1960s, owed their budgets to American companies – Warner Brothers, United Artists and others – and it was largely to the American backers that the profits went.

The James Bond films (beginning with *Doctor No* in 1962) were also made in Britain and brought movie stardom to Sean Connery – and, later, to Roger Moore – but they, too, were financed by Hollywood, as were David Lean's great successes of the 1960s, *Lawrence of Arabia* and *Dr Zhivago*. Stanley Kubrick settled in Britain to make *Lolita, Dr Strangelove* and *2001: A Space Odyssey*, but though these offered employment to British actors and technicians they were not, in any real (which is to say financial) sense, British films. Again, the movies were made in Britain; and again the profits, if any, went to America.

Throughout the decade the British industry lived in a fool's paradise. Yes, there was a great deal of production going on; yes, there was a kind of 'new wave' of writers, directors and performers that loosened the hitherto tight grip of the middle-class Establishment and showed, through the promotion of people with regional and London accents – people like Finney and Caine – that the working classes had far more to offer the movies than mere comic relief; and, yes, there was an abundance of gifted people in Britain.

But the euphoria induced by the fact that in 1968, for example, seventy-six feature films were made in Britain should have been counter-balanced by the sobering realisation that (as Alexander Walker again points out) more than sixty of them were wholly or partly financed in America. In 1969, perhaps realising the danger inherent in too much dependence on foreign money, EMI appointed the actor/writer/director Bryan Forbes as Head of Production at its Elstree Studios, thus making him probably the last tycoon of the British film industry. But though the experiment produced some notable films – Joseph Losey's *The Go-Between* among them – it was not a success and ended with Forbes's resignation two years later. Furthermore, though box-office takings rose during the decade, thanks to increased seat prices, cinema attendances, which had been as high as 30 million a week in 1945, declined sharply year by year to 4.7 million a week in 1969 and the number of cinemas in the country fell from more than 3,500 in 1959 to around 1,500 in 1970.

So when Hollywood, by now facing serious economic problems of its own and generally disappointed with the financial results accruing from its British investments, withdrew its support in the early 1970s, Britain's film industry was in a worse state than ever – a load of burgeoning talent on the one hand but a shrinking audience and a painful lack of money on the other.

In France, meanwhile, the cinema of the 60s was dominated by the new wave directors, Godard paramount among them. The early to middle years of the decade, when he made films like *The Little Soldier*, *Alphaville* and *Pierrot Le Fou*, were probably his best. Later, as he appeared to scorn anything as bourgeois as entertainment in favour of left-wing polemics, his work became ever more experimental and inaccessible, his bewildering *King Lear* in 1987, for example, being virtually impenetrable. Truffaut, too, continued to develop, starting with *Tirez sur le Pianiste* (*Shoot the Pianist*), following this with *Jules et Jim* and ending up with *L'Enfant Sauvage*, while Chabrol blossomed towards the end of the decade with two splendid thrillers, *La Femme Infidèle* and *Le Boucher.*

This was a bold and vigorous period for the French cinema. Alain Resnais aroused admiration and bafflement in just about equal measures with *Last Year at Marienbad*, a surrealist exercise in the manipulation of time, place and memory, and Robert Bresson confirmed his position as a sort of guru to the *nouvelle vague* directors with *The Trial of Joan of Arc*. In addition Buñuel returned to France to make, among other pictures, *Belle de Jour* and a veritable horde of younger directors beavering away and clamouring for attention included Louis Malle, Claude Lelouch, Erich Rohmer and Agnes Varda. And, of course, the pouting, sultry Brigitte Bardot was still purveying sex more raunchily than anyone else anywhere you care to name.

The strength of the French industry, *vis-à-vis* that of Britain, is that France doesn't have the handicap of sharing the same language with America. Consequently while British cinemas could easily get by – and sometimes seem positively eager to get by – without ever showing a single British film, French cinemas could not hope to survive by offering a menu of dubbed or subtitled American pictures alone. Besides, I doubt if Gallic patriotism would allow it; the French are by no means averse to Hollywood movies but being, along with virtually every other European nation, far more interested in the cinema and far more aware of its importance as an art form than the British are, they also support their own films.

The Italians, too, got along very well in the 1960s without excessive injections of American production money. Fellini had moved into his flamboyant period with *La Dolce Vita* in 1959 and continued in similar or even more extravagant vein with *8½* and *Satyricon*. Visconti became ever more theatrical as he progressed from *Rocco and His Brothers* in 1960 to *The Damned* in 1970; Michelangelo Antonioni featured the stunning Monica Vitti in *L'Avventura, La Notte* and *Red Desert* as well as taking a trip to England to film *Blow-Up*; Bernardo Bertolucci arrived dramatically on the scene, especially with *Before the Revolution*; and Claudia Cardinale joined Vitti and Sophia Loren (not forgetting Bardot, of course) in the ranks of international sexpots.

The German cinema took longer than others in Europe to recover from the effects of war. Its true renaissance was to come later but at the end of the 1960s there were encouraging signs that things were looking up. Rainer Werner Fassbinder, described by the American critic Vincent

Canby as 'the most original talent since Godard', made an energetic entry on the scene with three films in 1969 including *Katzelmacher* and *Love Is Colder than Death*, by which time the controversial Werner Herzog, a kind of romantic visionary-cum-masochist who appears to insist on making his films in the most difficult and dangerous circumstances possible, was already becoming established with four pictures to his credit, including *Signs of Life*.

Throughout the 60s the dominant figure in Sweden was again the industrious Ingmar Bergman, who made thirteen films during the decade, among them *Through a Glass Darkly, The Silence* and *Persona*. In addition, Mai Zetterling, hitherto known almost exclusively as an actress, turned feature director with *Loving Couples, Night Games* and *The Girls* and Bo Widerberg made, among other films, the beautifully photographed *Elvira Madigan*. But perhaps the Swedish director who most caught the eye – and certainly the headlines – was Vilgot Sjoman, whose *I Am Curious: Yellow* and *I Am Curious: Blue* (these being the colours of his national flag) were so sexually explicit as to be regarded at the time as virtually pornographic. Naturally, they both found a lucrative international market.

In Denmark the venerable Carl Dreyer, one of the most respected of movie pioneers, who had been making films since 1912, completed a distinguished career with *Gertrud*, which many regard as a masterpiece, and soon afterwards died at the age of 79.

Meantime, behind what was then known as the 'Iron Curtain', Czechoslovakia produced Milos Forman (*A Blonde in Love* and *The Fireman's Ball*) but very soon lost both him and another talented debutant, Ivan Passer, to Hollywood. The Polish industry suffered a similar fate when Roman Polanski, having made his presence felt with *Knife in the Water*, promptly high-tailed it for Britain and Jerzy Skolimowski followed his much-admired *Le Départ*, a Golden Bear winner at the Berlin festival, by departing himself, eventually for the same destination as Polanski. However, Andrzej Wajda – director of *Ashes and Diamonds* and *Man of Marble* – who was better than either of them, stayed in Warsaw. In Russia, meanwhile, the 1960s saw the advent of that country's most gifted modern director, Andrei Tarkovsky, whose *Solaris* in 1972 was to bring him worldwide recognition.

Much further to the east, the Indian film industry continued to be hugely prolific, although to Western eyes it sometimes seemed to consist solely of Satyajit Ray, who followed his splendid 'Apu' trilogy with films like *Devi* and *Kanchenjunga*. In Japan the two acknowledged masters, Kon Ichikawa and Akira Kurosawa, continued to be highly productive either as writers or directors or both. Ichikawa, for instance, made *Alone on the Pacific, An Actor's Revenge* and the documentary *Tokyo Olympiad*, while amongst Kurosawa's contributions were *Yojimbo* (later ripped off and remade as the spaghetti western *A Fistful of Dollars*) and *Red Beard*. Of the heirs presumptive to these two the most significant was Nagisa Oshima, whose *Death by Hanging* was an outspoken examination of the treatment accorded to Koreans in Japan.

In America, with the old moguls like Louis Mayer of MGM and Harry Cohn of Columbia now dead, and Jack Warner soon to step aside as head of Warner Brothers, the 60s were quite as much a time of transition as the 50s had been. The studios were swiftly taken over by multinational companies and moved increasingly into TV as well as film production. And as the moguls passed, so did the great directors. In 1965 John Ford made his last film, *Seven Women*; Raoul Walsh rounded off his own career in 1964 with *A Distant Trumpet*; Michael Curtiz's swansong was *The Commancheros* in 1962; and Howard Hawks called it a day after *Rio Lobo* in 1970.

Now, with what was left of the studios being run not, as in the past, by men who loved money and movies in equal measure but by lawyers and accountants who read balance sheets rather than scripts, the creative power was falling increasingly into the hands of the stars and their agents. These were the people who could put packages and deals together, thus saving the business and law school graduates currently in charge of the industry from having to make difficult decisions in areas of which they knew nothing. At the same time, the rising generation of directors – Sidney Lumet, for example, Sydney Pollack, George Roy Hill, Arthur Penn and John Frankenheimer – had mostly learnt their trade in television rather than the cinema. The break with the golden age was pretty well complete, except perhaps at 20th Century Fox where Darryl F. Zanuck, who had been Head of Production from 1934 to 1956 before leaving to become an independent producer, was brought back to take command in 1962. Of all the studios it was predominantly Fox that tried to cling on to the vanishing family audience. That company's huge success with *The Sound of Music* in 1965 encouraged it to believe that what people really wanted in the cinema was musicals. Wrong. They may certainly have wanted *The Sound of Music* as well as Disney's *Mary Poppins* and Warners' *My Fair Lady* but, as they indicated by staying at home in huge numbers, they did not want *Dr Dolittle*, or *Star!* or even Barbra Streisand in *Hello, Dolly*.

By now the children of the postwar baby boom had come of cinema-going age and their tastes were not those of their parents. These after all were the Swinging Sixties, an era of permissiveness, demos, youthful rebellion and Vietnam, and this younger generation was looking for films that reflected the mood and emotions of the time. Penn caught that mood with *Bonnie and Clyde*, Dennis Hopper with *Easy Rider*, Sam Peckinpah with *The Wild Bunch*, Mike Nichols with *The Graduate*, George Roy Hill with *Butch Cassidy and the Sundance Kid*.

Hollywood produced some fine movies in the 1960s but it was nevertheless a time of great confusion. What used to work at the box office no longer did or even more bafflingly (as in the case of the musicals) only worked sometimes. The old Hollywood had gone and with it the values it had tried to sustain.

In 1960 the Oscar for best film went to Billy Wilder's *The Apartment*, a mordant, cynical comedy in which Jack Lemmon lets out his apartment to philandering colleagues to further his ambition to gain a cherished key to the executive washroom. It was regarded as somewhat risqué at the time but as sex and violence came ever more to dominate the movies it began to seem increasingly tame. In 1969 the Oscar went to John Schlesinger's *Midnight Cowboy* in which Jon Voigt plays a country boy come to New York to offer sex for sale to lonely women. It seems an apt summing-up of the changes that had taken place in the previous ten years that *Midnight Cowboy* was the first X-rated film ever to win the Academy Award.

Four – Juveniles and Blockbusters

Around the middle of the 1970s everything changed again. Until then the same audiences that had flocked to the likes of *Bonnie and Clyde, The Graduate* and *Easy Rider* – none of which may exactly have stretched the boundaries of film too far but all of which contained at least a grain of thought and a modicum of comment on society – were still around. These were the audiences who, in 1970, brought success to Robert Altman's *M.A.S.H.*, a darkly funny, sometimes savage satire on the Korean War, and in 1972 made *The Godfather*, directed by Francis Coppola (or do I mean Francis Ford Coppola? Difficult to tell. He seems to have two names or three depending on his mood), the most lucrative film of all time. Or anyway the most lucrative film of all time up to then; the qualification is important because, the way things went in the last five or six years of the 70s, such records didn't last long.

M.A.S.H. and *The Godfather* were not simply a black comedy and the most absorbing gangster movie ever made; they also had things to say about, respectively, the lunacy of war and the dark side of the American Dream. You didn't necessarily have to be a rocket scientist to appreciate either but it was at least advisable to keep your brain in gear.

But then in 1975 the 28-year-old Steven Spielberg directed *Jaws*, a cracking good movie to be sure and superbly made but one which, at the same time, aspired to be nothing more than entertainment, sheer escapism. And a whole new audience was discovered, a much younger audience aged roughly between 12 and 24. They were interested neither in subtexts nor in political or social messages; what they wanted was action, excitement, thrills, violence, sex and laughs. Immediately *Jaws* became the most lucrative film ever made – a title it was to hold but briefly – and Hollywood, never slow to scramble aboard a bandwagon, began to cater for, or rather pander to, this new, young and undemanding breed of cinemagoer.

Thus the 'Movie Brats' were born, the Movie Brats being a generic name bestowed liberally – and, in retrospect, rather nonsensically – upon a whole group of film makers who in fact had very little in common except that they were all roughly of an age, came to prominence about the same time and were successful. Spielberg was a Movie Brat, so were George Lucas (who directed *Star Wars* and produced the 'Indiana Jones' movies), Martin Scorsese, John Carpenter (especially after *Halloween*) and Brian De Palma. Many of these were film-school graduates, others came from television, most of them were born during or after the Second World War and – one thing they did tend to have in common – they had been brought up in an audio-visual, rather than a literary, environment. Spielberg, for instance, once confessed to me that he was not a man to curl up with a good book, while Scorsese told me that so far as he could recall there were no books in his home at all until he himself, aged 15, introduced works by Thomas Hardy and Graham Greene. Even Coppola was lumped in with these Movie Brats, though mostly because he was a kind of guru for the others. In fact Coppola was a much more cultured man than his younger associates: he had been raised in a household where all the arts were respected and studied; his father, Carmine, was an Oscar-winning composer and he himself won three Oscars for best screenplay (*Patton*, *The Godfather* and *The Godfather Part II*) and another for directing *The Godfather Part II*. No doubt he was admired by his near-contemporaries and disciples for his erudition, but what they mostly respected was his track record as a film maker and his reputation as the man who had bucked the system by creating (ultimately unsuccessfully) his own studio, Zoetrope, one of whose aims was to give himself and other like-minded directors and writers a measure of independence.

During the 70s the established studios – with the exception of Universal and Disney, both of which were also heavily involved in television production – had virtually abandoned film-making themselves and were concentrating on financing and distributing independent pictures. More than ever, power was falling into the hands of producers, directors, actors and agents, especially the latter, the deal makers. Agents, indeed, acquired such clout that some of them became heads of studios, until they realised that in the new Hollywood agents had even more power than studio heads. At the end of the 1980s the most important man in Hollywood was Mike Ovitz, chief honcho of the Creative Artists Agency. When the Japanese company Matsushita bought MCA/Universal for $6.6 billion Ovitz acted as the honest broker, the middle man, and reputedly received a $50 million commission for his trouble. Even in Hollywood, where nothing exceeds like excess, $50 million is still regarded as quite a tidy sum of money. As the saying goes in and around Beverly Hills: 'Blessed are the deal makers, for they shall inherit the earth.'

Of course, in Hollywood the name of the game had always been money. But suddenly films like *Jaws*, with international earnings of around $400 million, had shown that potentially the profits were incalculable. Better still, where once only the studios or the financial backers would have benefited, now lots of people had a chance to dip their bread in the gravy. For the first time since movies began, one film could make star, producer and director so wealthy that they need never work again. (So long, that is, as each had a sharp agent who had managed to swing a smart deal on their behalf). It was like the 1849 gold rush but without the effort: you put together a movie, the public liked it and, bingo, you were richer than you had ever dreamed you might become.

A case in point. In 1970 Arthur Hiller had directed *Love Story* – the saccharine-sweet romance of ill-fated Ali McGraw and Ryan O'Neal – not, he told me, because he believed in the story too much but because he needed the work. For his efforts he received a small fee plus points (a share in the gross take). Soon after the film was finished, and somewhat strapped for cash, he offered his points for sale for $50,000 but at such a high price nobody was interested. The word going around was that *Love Story* was unlikely to do much business anyway. Hiller was, perforce, obliged to hang on to his points himself, which was fortunate because eventually, so well did the picture do, they brought him $11 million.

From *Jaws* Spielberg certainly made considerably more, and what George Lucas's take-home pay was after the astonishing worldwide success of *Star Wars* – the new, post-*Jaws* box-office record holder – it's impossible even to guess. What was clear, however, was that if you geared your film to the right audience – a young, thrill-seeking audience – you virtually had a licence to print money and from *Jaws* onwards that is what Hollywood set out to do and continued to do right through to the 1990s.

Coining a clumsy but descriptive word, the director Peter Bogdanovich described the period from the mid-1970s onwards as the era of 'the juvenilisation' of the movies. It was a time when, on the whole, style seemed to be more important than content. Soundtracks were dominated by ear-splitting rock music, the music of the young; incessant, restless movement was passed off as action; the staple denouement of practically every thriller or adventure story was a wild chase or general mayhem.

And this was particularly true of the endless sequels which at times seemed to dominate the cinema.

Sequels were not invented in the 70s and 80s; they had been around in various forms – the 'Tarzan', 'Topper' and 'Thin Man' films, for example – certainly since talking pictures began. But now the whole industry appeared to be geared to the sequel. *Jaws* was followed by three sequels, *Halloween* by four, *Police Academy* by six and *Friday the Thirteenth* by seven, for heaven's sake. All of these, along with the various 'Nightmares on Elm Street', 'Porkys', 'Karate Kids' and others, were designed simply to cash in on the success of the original film and not noticeably to develop or improve upon it. In many cases – *Jaws*, obviously, *Halloween*, Wes Craven's *A Nightmare on Elm Street* – the originals had been excellent examples of the genres from which they sprang. The sequels, however, sometimes looking more like straight remakes than follow-ups, brought the inevitable law of diminishing returns into play, guaranteeing that each chapter in the continuing, or if you prefer interminable, story was cruder and worse than the one that went before; and usually invention was so lacking that nobody could even be bothered to think up new titles, so that each episode had the same name as the first film with a number slapped after it.

The outstanding exception to this rule was *The Godfather Part II*, a film which was very different from and yet in its own way quite as good as the original. It had the advantage, of course, of having the same director, Coppola, and the same star, Al Pacino, as its predecessor, although continuity of personnel is no guarantee of quality in sequels.

Rocky, for example, was a perfectly decent little movie which won an Oscar for its director, John Avildsen, and promoted its previously unknown protagonist, Sylvester Stallone, to superstardom. Six years later (in 1982) *First Blood* introduced Stallone as John Rambo, another action-man hero. Once again this was not at all a bad picture, which at least had something – if not necessarily anything very profound – to say about the emotional traumas suffered by Vietnam veterans. These two characters, Rocky and Rambo, made Stallone the biggest star in movies and he continued to play them until the beginning of the 1990s despite the very obvious fact that Rockies II-V and Rambos II and III were becoming increasingly ludicrous as, in the end, even the audience realised.

That Stallone stayed with Rocky and Rambo until the bottom of the barrel had been thoroughly scraped was due to the simple fact that sequels were safe. They gave the audience exactly what it had already shown it liked and they made money. Or at least they did until a new batch of 12–24-year-olds came along and demanded icons of their own. Thus as Stallone's popularity began to wane in the second half of the 1980s, Eddie Murphy replaced him as Hollywood's number one box-office superstar (largely on the strength of *Beverly Hills Cop* and its inevitable sequel), until Murphy himself was replaced in his turn by Arnold Schwarzenegger, another sequel merchant with *Terminator* and *Terminator 2*.

It is indicative of the period that the biggest international stars of world cinema should have attained their eminence by playing what were essentially cartoon characters. Their immediate predecessor, Clint Eastwood, may never have been an actor in the class of Robert De Niro or Gérard Depardieu but his popular screen creations – Dirty Harry, Josey Wales and the nameless spaghetti western hero – though larger than life were at least recognisable people. But the era that spawned Stallone and his successors was the era of *Superman* and eventually *Batman* 1, 2, 3 and 4 with, no doubt, more to come. It was also the era in which Freddie, the evil, immortal and supernatural villain of the 'Elm Street' nightmares became a household name, although the actor who played him (Robert Englund) remains virtually anonymous.

This was indeed the juvenilisation of the movies, a time when Hollywood pandered cynically, almost desperately, to the tastes and desires of the young and in so doing made the ultimately dangerous discovery that vast profits were to be derived from blockbusters. Now blockbusters – films that cost a great deal, usually run for at least a couple of hours and invariably involve loads of special effects and slam-bang action – can be a great deal of fun. The 'Star Wars' and 'Indiana Jones' trilogies, two of the three 'Back to the Future' pictures, a couple of the 'Superman' quartet, *Ghostbusters, Gremlins, Romancing the Stone* and a few others are enjoyable, well-made movies. But they are, when you get right down to it, entertainments for teenagers; except perhaps technically they don't do much to further the art of the cinema. Yet because they made so much money these were the kind of films on which the studios became increasingly and anxiously reliant, anxiously because though blockbusters made a lot they also cost a lot. Consequently, while a successful blockbuster guaranteed a healthy end-of-the-year balance sheet, a failed blockbuster could bring catastrophe. The disaster of *Heaven's Gate*, for example, was responsible for the demise of United Artists, while in

1987 another dreadful flop, *Ishtar*, caused financial panic at Columbia.

The two stars of *Ishtar*, Warren Beatty and Dustin Hoffman, were paid $5.5 million each; Beatty picked up a further $500,000 as a producer's fee; and the director, Elaine May, received $1.5 million. So before a single foot of film had been exposed the movie had cost $13 million – and such fees were by no means rare. By the late 80s the average cost of a modest, run-of-the-mill Hollywood-made comedy or thriller was around $18 million and rising. Today it's closer to $50 million – and stars' salaries are largely responsible.

What had happened was that as the studios were taken over to become merely the entertainment arms of multinational conglomerates – Columbia, for instance, was bought by Coca-Cola, then sold to Sony; Paramount has long been a part of Gulf and Western; and Matsushita, of course, has acquired MCA/Universal – the people making financial decisions were not themselves film makers. Now embarking on any movie is a risk since it can easily take two or three years from conception to opening night and nobody, not even the most experienced producer or director, can be sure how public taste might change in that time. So the money men began to demand what they called guarantees before they would agree to meet the budget. And though in the movies *nothing* can be guaranteed a star name was reckoned to be about as close as you could get. Never mind the story, have you got Eastwood? Or Stallone? Or Cruise? Or Streep? Or Streisand? Or DiCaprio? With that kind of thinking going on, a script with a well-known star attached to it from day one would probably be made; a better script without a star name would probably not. The stars and their agents used the power thus conferred upon them to make ever more outrageous demands, insisting not merely upon $5–$6 million up front ($12 million or even $15 million if you were a Stallone, a Murphy or Schwarzenegger at the height of your popularity or $20 million for Jim Carrey or Leonardo DiCaprio) but a percentage of the film's gross take as well – and I don't mean gross profit, I mean gross take; I mean that a percentage of the very first dollar paid over at the box office, and of every subsequent dollar, goes to the star. An actor with that sort of contract doesn't have to be too bothered whether his movie is a success or not. If he is on, let us say, one per cent of the gross and the film takes $50 million, well, the star walks away with an extra half-million on top of his original fee and if the picture had actually cost $60 million to make and the studio was going to take a financial beating, tough.

It was this kind of risky (for the studios) set-up that David Puttnam announced that he was going to change when, in 1986, he took over as chairman of Columbia Pictures. Budgets, he said, were escalating out of control; actors' salaries were much too high; agents had become far too powerful. In future Columbia would have no truck with agents who offered ready-made deals – script, star, director and producer all neatly packaged together, take it or leave it. In the thirteen months that he lasted at the studio Puttnam proved that what he advocated could be done. He brought the average cost of a Columbia picture down to $14.5 million – far lower than anyone else. Unfortunately, though some excellent films were made during his brief regime – *Hope and Glory*, *The Last Emperor* and *Someone to Watch Over Me* among them – he produced no blockbusters and consequently no fat profits. Furthermore, in some way he offended the actor Bill Murray so that the year's projected blockbuster, *Ghostbusters* 2, in which Murray was to star, was postponed until after Puttnam had left. He also offended Warren Beatty and Dustin Hoffman when, quite properly, he refused to throw good money after bad by launching an expensive advertising/publicity campaign for the awful *Ishtar* (which had been made under the aegis of his predecessor). And his – in my view – justified attacks on what he saw as the greed of Hollywood made him powerful enemies among agents and independent producers, who ganged up against him. The fact that his cost-cutting philosophy was strongly supported by the kind of directors and producers who wanted to make comparatively low-budget films for grown-up audiences was to no avail. Low-budget films for grown-ups were out of fashion; Puttnam had to go – and he went. With hindsight I believe his mistake was not in his thinking but in announcing what he planned to do before he had actually done it.

Within a few years, as suddenly even blockbusters were seen to be no longer a cast-iron assurance of vast and instant profits, it became clear that Puttnam's policy made admirable sense but by then it was too late.

One of the reasons why Puttnam was treated like some irritating latterday Cassandra was that from *Jaws* onwards the youth/blockbuster policy regularly earned Hollywood vast amounts of revenue every year for comfortably more than a decade. Films that took well over $100 million at the American box office alone became commonplace. If you add to that the income from overseas distribution, television sales and the video market, which had been expanding rapidly since the mid-1970s, you could end up with a veritable gold mine like *E.T.*, which, by the end of the 80s, had brought in, worldwide and from all manner of sources, something in excess of $700 million. Admittedly *E.T.* is no longer the reigning, all-time money-spinning champ (that accolade goes to *Titanic*) but earnings of $250 million and more were by no means uncommon. Indeed, stories of studio heads rejecting low-budget movies that were virtually guaranteed to return a $10 million profit because they were only interested in films that would make ten times as much are not entirely apocryphal. This morbid interest in money infected not only the studios but also the media and the public. The sums movies took at the box office on their opening weekends were vital and were published and studied like football scores or league tables. Anything less than about $12 million in the first two or three days was thought to be disastrous and films that failed to reach that kind of target were automatically perceived as flops, regardless of their quality. Audiences were thus educated to patronise only those pictures which had opened strong and to ignore the others and the studios felt compelled to spend vast sums on advertising, publicity and general hype to ensure that their productions did open strong. If that failed to work the movie was pretty well written off, no matter how much it had cost because, well, win some, lose some and there was always another blockbuster coming along to take up the slack and make up the losses.

And yet, surprisingly perhaps in the circumstances, some excellent films were made during this time of juvenilisation, often by independent companies and comparatively unheralded directors like Walter Hill (*48 Hours*, for instance) and Sidney Lumet (*Dog Day Afternoon* and *Q & A*). In addition, Coppola followed the first two 'Godfathers' with *Apocalypse Now*; Spielberg contributed *Close Encounters of the Third Kind*, and *E.T.*; Woody Allen turned out a whole body of impressive work ranging from *Sleeper* to *Love and Death* and *Annie Hall* and from *Manhattan* to *Hannah and Her Sisters* and *Crimes and Misdemeanours*; Oliver Stone emerged with *Salvador* and *Platoon*; and most emphatically of all Martin Scorsese entered the 1990s widely, if not indeed universally, recognised as the most gifted of modern American directors.

Mean Streets (1973) and *Taxi Driver* (1976) had shown him to be a film maker of unusual talent but alone among the so-called Movie Brats Scorsese fully consolidated his position during the 1980s, a decade which for him began with *Raging Bull*, continued with *The King of Comedy* and *The Last Temptation of Christ* and ended with *Goodfellas*. Controversy has attended him almost from the start, but this is an inevitable consequence of his refusal to shy away from confrontation in his choice of subject matter or to gloss over the fact that America is an exceedingly violent country.

His fellow Movie Brats, however, had not fared so well in the long term. Coppola has certainly made three great films but his work since *Apocalypse Now* in 1979 (and this includes *The Cotton Club* and *The Godfather Part III*) has been at best uneven – brilliant and flawed in equal measure. Spielberg continued to show the golden touch with his completion of the 'Indiana Jones' trilogy but in the 1980s he did rather better as a producer (*Back to the Future, Who Framed Roger Rabbit?*) than as a director. His two attempts at adult films, *The Color Purple* and *Empire of the Sun*, were both unconvincing and *Hook*, his updated version of *Peter Pan* which many people had hoped would be his *E.T.* of the 90s, was a disappointment. (Mind you, he has since conquered even greater heights than before with *Schindler's List* and *Saving Private Ryan*.) George Lucas, who gave up directing after the promising *American Graffiti* and *Star Wars*, completed the 'Star Wars' trilogy as a producer and, in a similar capacity, fared well in collaboration with Spielberg on the 'Indiana Jones' films, but also produced a gigantic flop in *Howard the Duck*, which rapidly became known as 'Howard the Turkey'. Brian De Palma, who began strongly with *Phantom of the Paradise* and *Carrie* then moved on to the dazzling but distasteful *Dressed to Kill*, stumbled with his remake of *Scarface*, recovered his balance splendidly with *The Untouchables* and was later seen reeling away from the wreckage of *The Bonfire of the Vanities*.

As the 1990s began the Movie Brats were moving into or towards their fifties and had become mature, for the most part successful and respected members of the film community. They were and remain an exceptionally talented, if disparate, bunch and the immediate future of Hollywood may depend to a large extent on how much that maturity is reflected in their films over the next decade or so.

Meanwhile the British film industry, largely inspired by David Puttnam, had flowered strongly, though briefly in the late 70s and early 80s. With pictures like *That'll Be the Day* and *Stardust, Bugsy Malone* and *Midnight Express, The Duellists, Chariots of Fire* and *The Killing Fields*, Puttnam had offered opportunities, gratefully received, to such talented directors as Michael Apted, Alan Parker, Ridley Scott, Hugh Hudson and Roland Joffe. But, alas, all of them have since been obliged to seek their fortunes in America, as too has Bill Forsyth, director of

Gregory's Girl and *Local Hero*. British films (notably Richard Attenborough's *Gandhi* and Puttnam/Hudson's *Chariots*), British actors and British technicians won numerous Oscars during the 1980s but all that success merely diverts attention from the worrying fact that increasingly what Britain had – certainly until the mid-1990s – was not so much a film industry as a TV film industry.

Though it is true that some of the most successful and sometimes imaginative films of the 1980s were made by British directors – *Someone to Watch Over Me* and *Thelma and Louise* (Ridley Scott); *Angel Heart* and *Mississippi Burning* (Alan Parker); *Top Gun* (Tony Scott); *Fatal Attraction* (Adrian Lyne) – they were all made for American studios.

Meanwhile, in the UK, Goldcrest, a company which had bravely tried to recreate a British presence in international cinema, finally collapsed after ill-advisedly investing far too much money in two consecutive flops, Hugh Hudson's *Revolution* and the musical *Absolute Beginners*. Puttnam, in his post-Columbia period, returned to Warner Brothers for the funding of *Memphis Belle*, Jeremy Thomas made his Oscar-winning *The Last Emperor* with foreign backing, John Cleese raised the budget for *A Fish Called Wanda* in America. By 1989 the number of feature films produced wholly in Britain had declined to twenty-seven and most of those were produced basically for television.

From elsewhere in the world the remarkable Akira Kurosawa, though into his seventies, directed two acknowledged masterpieces, *Kagemusha* and *Ran*; Ingmar Bergman contributed the epic *Fanny and Alexander* and soon afterwards, aged 68, declared that he would direct no more; Wim Wenders, Herzog and, too briefly, Fassbinder gave energy to the New German Cinema; Satyajit Ray continued to represent the Indian cinema to the rest of the world; Fellini was still productive but after his *Casanova* 1976 found less acclaim than before; and Gérard Depardieu, apparently starring in a film a week, sometimes gave the impression that he was the entire French film industry as well as proving himself to be one of the best screen actors in the world, his only peers being Robert De Niro and (in German films such as *Mephisto* and *Colonel Redl*, though not so much in English-language pictures where his opportunities are more limited) Klaus Maria Brandauer.

For a while towards the end of the 1970s the new, state- and government-aided Australian film industry, led by the likes of Peter Weir (*Picnic at Hanging Rock* and *Gallipoli*), Bruce Beresford (*Breaker Morant*) and Fred Schepisi (*The Devil's Playground* and *The Chant of Jimmy*

Blacksmith), had shown great and unusual promise. But these three, along with performers like Paul Hogan (whose essentially Australian *Crocodile Dundee* had been the international box-office hit of 1986) were, like their British counterparts and the Dutch director Paul Verhoeven (*Total Recall* and *Basic Instinct*) drawn inexorably to America, still the land of opportunity and big money.

For the capital of the movie world remained Hollywood, where attendances and box-office continued to rise throughout the 1980s and the blockbuster lingered on as the universal panacea, the single, certain cure for all other financial ills – until a curious thing happened with *Batman*.

This was the blockbuster hit of 1989, a strangely dark and muted version of the comic strip with Michael Keaton as a low-key Batman and only an outrageously hammy performance by Jack Nicholson as the Joker to enliven it. Nevertheless, it was a great popular success and Nicholson reputedly earned somewhere between $20 million and $50 million from his fee and his share of both the box-office revenue and the spin-off merchandising. By early 1991 the film had grossed $253.4 million from cinemas alone and had become number five in the all-time money-making list.

Since it had cost a (comparatively) mere $53.5 million, the natural assumption was that the film must be hugely in profit. But in March 1991, the *Los Angeles Times* reported that *Batman* was still $35.8 million in the red. Now how on earth could that be? Admittedly, distribution fees, negative costs, advertising and publicity budgets and interest on money borrowed often mean that a film's production budget can be multiplied by three before a penny profit is seen. Nevertheless, and assuming that true expenditure on the picture was around $160 million, it would still seem to need some extremely clever creative accountancy to announce with a straight face and not a hint of suppressed mirth that the movie had made a loss. The fact that even as these doleful figures were announced Warners were already preparing *Batman 2* made it particularly difficult for the general populace to take the studio's tale of woe seriously.

But within the industry it *was* taken seriously because the interpretation was that, however the final balance sheet might come out, even a film as successful as *Batman* had not proved to be the guaranteed, licence-to-print-money, one-hundred-per-cent-profit maker that everyone had assumed. The bubble of the blockbuster had finally burst.

But not, as we will see, for long.

Five – Types of Uncertainty

In December 1989 in a television programme reviewing the films of the 80s, I delivered myself of this statement: 'It seems to me that the cinema is in a much better state than it was ten years ago. It's a long way from perfect, God knows. It still pays too little attention to plot, characterisation and dialogue. It still talks down to an audience which it believes is unable to concentrate for more than two minutes at a time and can be fobbed off with the flash and empty techniques of the pop video. But I do believe there's a growing awareness that this must change, that an older audience will increasingly be a more demanding audience.'

Well, I got that wrong.

Now, three years into the cinema's second century, the situation – certainly as far as the major Hollywood movies are concerned – is probably worse than it was in 1989. Of course, looking at the recent strength of America's independent sector and the British film industry, you could argue that this doesn't matter too much. You could even ask why I think Hollywood pictures are so important anyway.

Very well then. The American independents have indeed produced some excellent stuff in recent years. From the Coen brothers, for example, we had *Fargo*; from Tim Robbins *Dead Man Walking*; from Britain's Mike Figgis, working under nerve-wracking conditions, often without permission to film in the streets, there came *Leaving Las Vegas*; Saul Zaentz, with the aid of the English writer-director Anthony Mingella, gave us *The English Patient*.

Each of these won critical acclaim along with a respectable degree of financial success and an Oscar or two – in the case of *The English Patient*, nine. Meanwhile, from the currently resurgent British industry (of which more later) came such splendidly crafted and popular films as *Four Weddings And a Funeral*, *The Madness of King George*, Mike Leigh's *Secrets and Lies*, Danny Boyle's *Trainspotting* and *The Full Monty*, the first and last of which could in turn claim to be the most lucrative British picture ever made.

What they all, American and British alike, had in common was that they sprang from well-written screenplays; none was reliant on special effects or state of the art technology. And, thanks to this, for a little while – a very little while – it began to look as if we were on the verge of a significant change in the industry. At the 1997 Academy Awards ceremony when *The English Patient* and *Fargo* won their prizes the Oscars for best actor (Geoffrey Rush in the Australian film *Shine*) and best adapted screenplay (Billy Bob Thornton for *Slingblade*) also went to independent productions. The only Hollywood studio film even in contention was Columbia's *Jerry Maguire* and all it came away with was Cuba Gooding's trophy for best supporting actor.

At the end of the evening I asked David Ansen, the film critic of *Newsweek* magazine, for his reaction to these surprising events. What they indicated to him, he said, was that the very people who worked in the American industry – in other words, the bulk of the Academy's 5,300 or so voters – were telling Hollywood that they were fed up with the kind of juvenile movies that the studios were producing, that they wanted something better, meatier, more challenging.

The question was: would this protest – if that's what it was – be sustained?

Flash forward twelve months to the Awards ceremony of 1998 and we had the answer. James Cameron's *Titanic*, the archetypal Hollywood blockbuster, equalled the record of *Ben-Hur* by winning eleven Oscars. Was it then the best film of the year? By no means – Curtis Hanson's police thriller *L.A. Confidential* was but it, like *The Full Monty*, had to be content with consolation prizes, while Ang Lee's *The Ice Storm*, an outstandingly intelligent and evocative recreation of America in the 70s, failed even to gain a nomination.

The Academy members' rebellion of 1997 had lamely fizzled out and pretty well right down the line they voted American possibly, I think, from a sense of relief. With an estimated budget of close to $250 million *Titanic* – which contrives to be very impressive without actually being very good – is the most expensive film ever made. If, as was widely feared before its release, it proved to be a flop its backers, Paramount and in particular 20th Century Fox, would have faced embarrassing financial problems, which could in turn have had a knock-on effect for the entire industry. But it wasn't a flop – indeed it rapidly became the first film ever to rake in more than $1 billion at the box office alone. So not only were Fox and Paramount saved, but the whole of Hollywood felt itself to have had a narrow escape and, I suspect, decided to show its gratitude at Oscar time.

In the American industry the bottom line is always the dollar. The important fact that David Ansen and I had overlooked in the euphoria of the 1997 Oscar results was that while, at the time of the awards, *The English Patient* had taken $65 million at the box office, *Jerry Maguire* had taken $120 million. Columbia might have envied some of *The English Patient's* Oscars but wouldn't have swapped a dollar of revenue for any one of them. For when you come right down to it, awards are all very well, but movie making is a business and in business money speaks louder than anything else. After all, while your personal tastes might run to a cordon bleu restaurant with a small clientele you wouldn't necessarily invest in it if you had the chance instead to put your savings into Macdonalds, where everyone eats. So in 1998, maybe even a little scared by their own boldness a year ago, the Academy members lined up solidly behind *Titanic*, the Macdonalds of the movies.

I don't wish to belabour *Titanic* too much; for what it is it's well done and once the ship starts to sink you cannot help but be impressed by the sheer size and ingenuity of the special effects. But that's only half the film; the other half – the love story involving Kate Winslet, the first-class passenger, and Leonardo DiCaprio, travelling steerage – is sheer banality, an uninspired tale calculatedly designed by Cameron, the writer, to enable Cameron, the director, to show as much of his huge model of the ship as possible. Thus the film owed its success largely to its state of the art technology, plus the number of pubescent girls who went back time and again to lust after DiCaprio, and hardly at all to its screenplay, which, despite the general goodwill surrounding the picture, wasn't even deemed worthy of an Oscar nomination.

And that, I fear, is the template which, given *Titanic's* astonishing success, Hollywood will eagerly adopt as we move towards the new millennium: a hot star name surrounded by ever more elaborate special effects and if the screenplay isn't up to much, who cares?

Hardly a new concept, to be sure, and yet ironically one which at the beginning of the 1990s seemed to have run its course. For then the most successful films – *Dances With Wolves* and *The Silence of the Lambs*, for instance – though admittedly big and expensive offered decent scripts and plot and character development. Meanwhile, the traditional blockbusters, those dependent on starry names and action rather than a well-fashioned script, fared badly. Tom Cruise had an unaccustomed flop with *Days of Thunder*, as did Jack Nicholson with *The Two Jakes*, a sequel to *Chinatown*; Bruce Willis flopped twice with the dire *The Bonfire of the Vanities* and the inane *Hudson Hawk*. Eddie Murphy had a failure with *Another 48 Hours* and so did Julia Roberts with *Sleeping With the Enemy*.

For a while there the traditional blockbuster was failing to deliver; and if that were not bad enough there was the shock revelation provided by the economic recession of the early 90s that, for the first time, even the movies weren't depression-proof. In 1989 box office receipts in America had hit a record high of $5 billion; by 1991 they had fallen to $3.9 billion.

As a result Hollywood was in confusion. Blockbusters were collapsing and dying on the starting line, while the movies that delivered were comparatively small and comparatively cheap. At the box office the likes of *Ghost*, *Pretty Woman* and *Home Alone* were outperforming the megabucks movies. In this state of flux nobody knew any longer which bandwagon to leap upon; nobody even knew where the bandwagons were.

Companies like MGM, Orion and Carolco (later to file for bankruptcy) were in deep financial trouble. Paramount and Disney urgently needed hits, Columbia Tri-Star and Universal wondered anxiously how much longer their Japanese masters would be content to sit back watching more money pour out than poured in without adopting a hands-on policy towards film production.

Economy had become the order of the day. In December 1991, Steven Spielberg told *Premiere* magazine: 'I feel really privileged that I was given a chance to make *Hook* at a critical time in our industry, when everybody is trying to figure out how to tighten their belts.' The point was well made. *Hook*'s budget had crept up from an estimated $40 million to $70 million and more, at which point Spielberg, along with the stars, Dustin Hoffman and Robin Williams, agreed to defer their salaries and take instead a greater share of the gross box-office receipts. And this, as Spielberg also remarked to *Premiere*, at a time when 'certain studios that I'm very involved with have suddenly said, "We're only going to make one megamovie a year as opposed to three."'

So that was what it had come down to – budgets, and the number of megamovies, slashed; studio staff laid off. A leaner, paler Hollywood had begun to peer nervously out at the world around it. Even the stars' salaries, though not exactly cut, were at least for a while stabilised.

Of course, it couldn't – and didn't – last. Yet, coincidentally or not, in this period of comparative belt-tightening the quality of Hollywood films improved. In 1992 the Oscars for best film and best director went to Clint Eastwood's magnificent, revisionist western *Unforgiven*. (Other awards were conferred upon equally intelligent and thoughtful films such as Neil Jordan's *The Crying Game* and the Ismael Merchant-James Ivory production, *Howard's End,* but these, of course, were independent productions.) The following year Spielberg finally gained the Academy recognition that he had long – and wrongfully – been denied when he and *Schindler's List* won seven awards.

Meanwhile, during Hollywood's period of relative unease, excellent films were being produced in other parts of the world. Jane Campion's serious and uncompromising Antipodean production *The Piano* (which, frankly, I admired far more than I liked) won three Oscars. Indeed, there was good stuff from all over. China contributed Zhang Yimou's *Raise the Red Lantern* and *The Story of Qiu Ju*; Belgium provided *Toto the Hero* and the wicked black comedy, *Man Bites Dog*; France chipped in with *The Hairdresser's Husband* and Sweden with Billie August's *The Best Intentions*, from Ingmar Bergman's screenplay about his parents; while in Britain Ken Loach made the political comedy *Raining Stones* and the excellent *Land and Freedom* and Kenneth Branagh the rip-roaring *Much Ado About Nothing*.

But then economic conditions improved and the studios reaffirmed their faith in the kind of expensive popcorn movies they really preferred. *Forrest Gump* won numerous Oscars in 1994 and *Braveheart* was deemed best picture of 1995. By December 1996 the highly respected writer-director David Mamet was complaining that when asked what a Hollywood screen writer actually did these days, he was pretty well stuck for an answer.

For now the blockbuster was back, bigger, more expensive and for the most part emptier even than before. Spielberg led the way with *Jurassic Park*, a marvel of special effects hung on the most slender of plots, which swiftly became the most lucrative film ever made and remained so until *Titanic* came along. Kevin Costner chipped in with the $175 million *Waterworld*, which, though a critical disaster, did finally recoup its cost. Then came *Twister, Independence Day, Mars Attacks!*, two more *Batman* movies and a sequel to *Jurassic Park*.

All of these and many more depended almost entirely on visual spectacle and state of the art technology hung on a perfunctory story with a minimum of characterization and dialogue. Thus they confirmed the theory of Professor Marc Crispin Miller of Johns Hopkins University, Baltimore, that as films increasingly become industrial products in the market place the makers 'home in on the most infantile human needs, turning out in effect reassuring comic strips with high sex and violence contents.'

So, despite the odd glitch of the 1997 Oscar awards, the answer to the question: what does a Hollywood screen writer do these days is simple – he merely joins the dots between one action sequence and another using as few words as possible and eschewing any idea that might cause the audience to shift its brain into gear.

Now why should this be? Because the people who make the films are fools? By no means. They and their bosses are in fact very shrewd. American, especially Hollywood, pictures now dominate the world market more than ever before. In Britain and Germany upwards of 90 per cent of the films shown are made in the USA; even in the more chauvinistic France the figure exceeds 60 per cent and, since the fall of the Communist regimes and the collapse of their state-subsidised film industries, Hollywood has been exerting a considerable grip on cinema audiences in Eastern Europe, too, as well as making significant inroads into the markets in China and the Far East.

Europe now provides about 40 per cent of Hollywood's revenue and the rest of the world is beginning to add its own, by no means unimportant, contribution. But ... the great majority of that foreign audience is far from fluent in English and cannot be expected to sit through films that are heavily reliant on complexities of plot and subtle dialogue. While dubbing circumvents the problem in some countries it's not applicable everywhere.

On the other hand everyone can understand and even enjoy action, sex, mayhem and dazzling special effects, especially if the dialogue is spare and the storyline is simple and pared to the bone. Hence the new, easy to digest blockbusters – the international junk food of the cinema. To underline the popularity of such fare, the box-office take in America in 1997 had risen to $6.5 billion (and that before *Titanic* had properly opened), while in Britain in the same year cinema attendances – which had fallen below 50 million in the early 1980s – rose to 139.3 million. True, the British figure was boosted by the popularity of *The Full Monty,* but for the most part it was American films that drew the biggest audiences.

Yet not all is gloom. My stock answer when people complain that films aren't as good as they used to be has always been that in fact they are – and, incidentally, are also quite as bad as they used to be — and I see no reason to change that. We remember the best films of the past because, by and large, they are the ones that are re-released on video and shown on television. The worst are mercifully forgotten.

Therefore, if you look beyond the present dross there is still much cause for optimism. The likes of Woody Allen, Spielberg and Scorsese, along with Bob and Harvey Weinstein at Miramax, continue to make or promote films that demand intelligent appreciation. The brothers Joel and Ethan Coen, to their credit, have no truck with commercialism and improve all the time. Extremely well-made mainstream pictures like *The Usual Suspects* and *L.A. Confidential* crop up at regular intervals to surprise and delight us. And we must not forget the phenomenon of the 1990s, Quentin Tarantino, whose first two movies, *Reservoir Dogs* and *Pulp Fiction*, dramatically reshaped the crime thriller.

With a projected box-office take for 1998 which should exceed that of the previous year, the cinema in America is in a healthy condition and now the studios are taking a proprietorial interest in independent production (Miramax, for instance, nestles under the wing of Disney) there could be greater encouragement and opportunity for young film makers who seek to do something different and better.

In the rest of the world, too, things are looking up. There are signs of a resurgence in the French and German industries; in a too brief career Krzysztof Kieslowski reminded us of the underlying strength of the Polish cinema; Chen Kaige, along with Zhang Yimou and others, produced some startling work in China; Jane Campion, Gillian Armstrong and Baz Luhrmann (who followed *Strictly Ballroom* with the dazzling pyrotechnics of his contemporary *Romeo and Juliet*) maintain a strong Australian contribution, and from New Zealand have come *Heavenly Creatures* – which introduced Kate Winslet to the screen – and the bitterly effective *Once Were Warriors*.

Meanwhile, thanks in part to a new and more sympathetic government, Britain is enjoying a boom such as the country has not seen since the 1960s and one which, with a little care and thought, promises to last. The injection of money from the National Lottery and the introduction of tax breaks, which enable producers to write off the cost of a film in one year rather than three, should help provide the industry with a sound financial base. It is greatly – though not entirely – encouraging that 124 films were made in Britain in 1997 as opposed to 23 in 1989.

Not entirely encouraging? No, because by the end of 1997 more than 40 British pictures were still lying on producers' shelves awaiting a distribution deal. Most of them were cheaply made but nevertheless the total investment was too high to be ignored. The industry cannot afford to make films on spec and in the often unwarranted hope that distribution will undoubtedly follow.

It won't, especially as statistics prove that indigenous audiences overwhelmingly prefer American (i.e. Hollywood) films to the home-made variety. The Government's Film Policy Review Board has been and still is looking into this problem with the aim of establishing a more equitable distribution deal for British product. Such a thing is long overdue, but the suggestion, at least implicit in the Review Board's report, that in future the local industry might be distribution, rather than production, led is fraught with danger. A policy under which films were made not because the makers believed in them but because distributors could find a market for them would lead to the kind of dumbing down that has plagued Hollywood.

Producers of, say, *Five Weddings and a Christening* or *The Full Monty – And Then Some* would probably do well, but those who wished to make something original would be squeezed out and the creative energy which has led to the current boom in Britain would rapidly disappear. Undoubtedly some kind of balance must be struck between the desires of producers and the demands of distributors but it must be a balance, which is to say fair to both sides. If such a solution can be found the future of the British film industry seems assured for some time to come.

And apart from that, how do we sum up as the millennium approaches? Well, in 1998 the Oscar for best actor went to the 61-year-old Jack Nicholson rather than Robert Duvall (68), Dustin Hoffman (61) or Peter Fonda (59). The only nominee not galloping up towards his bus pass was 27-year-old Matt Damon, which doesn't say a lot for the ascendancy of youth.

What's more, Hollywood's current glamour queens are Kim Basinger (45), Michelle Pfeiffer and Sharon Stone (both 41) and the comparatively youthful Demi Moore (36 and currently the highest-paid woman in films, having received $12 million for the frightful *Striptease*.) None, however, has anything like the supremacy enjoyed in previous decades by Jane Fonda and Meryl Streep.

There are, however, younger people coming up. Julia Roberts, at 31, is still there or thereabouts and the likes of Matt Damon, Gwyneth Paltrow, Alicia Silverstone and Cameron Diaz have their admirers. Britain, too, is contributing its share of likely newcomers with such as Ewan McGregor, Kate Winslet and Robert Carlyle. But generally speaking it's the older performers who hold sway right now, the careers of Peter Fonda and the 62-year-old Burt Reynolds, for example, having apparently been revived by *Ulee's Gold* and *Boogie Nights* respectively.

Mind you, neither has enjoyed quite such a resurrection as John Travolta, who, after his musical successes of the 1970s, was pretty well forgotten until Tarantino and *Pulp Fiction* brought him so triumphantly back from the cinematic dead that he was able to join Jim Carrey in that exclusive band of actors who could demand $20 million a picture.

When the first edition of this book appeared in 1992 the biggest, most expensive star in the world – rubbing along on precious little more than $15 million a movie – was Arnold Schwarzenegger, a man who is not so much an actor as a human special effect. And I wondered then what the Lumière brothers might think if they knew their magical invention had laboured for a hundred years only to bring forth a Schwarzenegger.

Well, the question is no longer applicable. On the eve of the millennium Arnie has been toppled as the biggest star in the world to be replaced not by Travolta or Carrey but by Leonardo DiCaprio, whose presence in the cast accounted for so much of the popularity of *Titanic* and pretty well the entire box-office success of that very ordinary swashbuckler, *The Man in the Iron Mask*. Never mind that in the latter he was acted off the screen by Jeremy Irons and Gabriel Byrne: it was DiCaprio who drew teenage girls in their hordes to the cinemas.

And so as the financial belts that were tightened so rigorously, albeit briefly, in the early 1990s are once more let out a notch or two it's DiCaprio who, we are told, will set up a new record by being paid $25 million for his next picture. God alone knows where this will all end just as He alone knows to what heights future movie budgets will soar.

On Oscar night 1998 I asked Bill Mechanic, head of 20th Century Fox, if his studio would ever again invest in a $250 million movie. 'No way,' he said firmly. But, rest assured, some other studio will. Already movie budgets and star salaries have soared to such an extent that the sums involved seem to have more relevance to the world of Mickey Mouse than real life.

And, as history has taught us, they will undoubtedly increase while sane people look on aghast and say, 'This must surely be the end' and will be wrong, as they always have been. To those who claim that less is more Hollywood replies that more is better and therefore ever greater sums will be paid out in the hope of recouping even greater revenue.

In any other business this might seem a perilously risky strategy to adopt but the cinema is not like any other business and anyway Hollywood's bizarre economic policy seems to have worked so far. So as they advance into the 21st century, the movies, I predict, will survive, maybe in a different form, maybe one day on the Internet or something similar rather than in cinemas, but as gross and excessive and infuriating and enchanting as they have always been. Every year a handful of them will be profitable enough to compensate, and more, for the losses of the others and in among all the crap there will be the odd gleam of gold that continually encourages us in the belief that here, truly, is the art form of the modern age.

Six – A Question of Choice

Passion is to be found in the most unexpected places. Who, for example, would have thought that the Official Receiver's office could nurture a man whose devotion to the cinema was such that for twenty years he spent his free time compiling a list of all the films ever made anywhere in the world? Yet such a man is Alan Goble and he has published his findings in two huge volumes called *The International Film Index*. It contains 232,000 entries and, never mind the fact that inevitably his book was out of date even as he was delivering it to his publisher, I salute him.

And at this stage I might as well admit that I, personally, have not seen all 232,000 films and what's more I'm not at all sorry. On Mr Goble's list there are certainly many pictures that I wish I had seen, but there are many thousands more that I'm desperately glad I haven't because most of them, like most books, plays, TV programmes or music, will range from the barely tolerable to utter rubbish. In truth, I have no idea how many movies I have enjoyed, sat through or just suffered, although at a conservative estimate it must be well in excess of 10,000 – not a lot perhaps when set against 232,000, but even so I reckon I must have spent the best part of two years of my life merely sitting in a cinema. Is this really a job for a grown man? There are times when, enduring the likes of *The Omen IV* or *Rocky V* or *The Bonfire of the Vanities*, I have serious doubts.

The point is, however, that the list which follows this chapter is as much influenced by the films I haven't seen as those I have. It is also, of course, entirely personal not only because for me that was the fun of it but also because there is no such thing as a definitive roster of the 100 best films ever made. All criticism is subjective and in a sense everyone who watches a film – with the exception of those who choose to leave their brains in neutral – is a critic, with opinions about what he/she has just seen. It could be argued that any movie you have enjoyed is a good movie, or at least it was for you, so who cares what professional critics think? I don't altogether go along with that, although I will proffer the suggestion that all professional critics are parasites in that they live off other people's work. But to that I would also add the rider that parasites can be useful; they can clean the infection from wounds and that's what critics as parasites should do. They should have enough experience, knowledge, understanding and taste (though taste, too, is subjective) to recognise and identify excellence and its obverse when they see them. By so doing they can in a small way, and always assuming anyone is paying attention, play their part in helping to maintain standards.

A film is not necessarily good simply because it happened to divert or entertain you for a while. A film can only start to be good if all its individual parts – the story, the script, the acting, direction, production values (costumes, sets, special effects, choice of locations, etc.), cinematography, editing and music – are good, although that doesn't necessarily mean unflawed. The plot of *Casablanca*, for instance, is grossly flawed. All that stuff about a wartime escape route through Casablanca is total nonsense; no such thing existed but that doesn't mean the movie is not a good one – it is indeed a great one. Because *Casablanca*, like all classic films, has that vital but indefinable extra quality, the result perhaps of a kind of chemical reaction that occurs when all the components blend so well that somehow, good as the individual parts may be, the whole is even better.

But if all those things merely make a good film, what constitutes a great film? In Hollywood they talk of a movie having 'legs' and by that they mean one that opens strongly at the box office and continues to do well throughout its initial run. But these are the short legs, sprinters' legs if you like. Far more important are the legs that keep a film going for decades or even generations. Films equipped with legs like that, the legs of a marathon runner, are the ones that qualify not just as hits of the moment but as classics, for they have the additional attribute of timelessness.

In many cases this stems from having somehow encapsulated the general in the particular, of having hit upon a universal and eternal truth and held it up to the light for all to recognise and examine. There are many films like that in this book; but there are also others which have a different kind of timelessness. They may not say anything of profound importance about the human condition but they have the power to enchant and entertain one generation after another; for that reason they are classic movies, great movies and in its own way each of them, like all the others in the list, is a work of art.

And yet ... throwing around words like 'great', 'classic' and 'art' is a tricky business because where you stick these labels is a highly personal matter. More than that, it always seems to me to be a sort of minor miracle when a film comes along that deserves such appellations. A few years ago in New York I was talking to David Mamet. He was then in the process of editing *House of Games*, the first film he had directed, and being no doubt aware that he had something pretty hot on his hands, he was in bullish mood.

During the conversation, and thinking of the process of film-making and of the variety of people – not all of them by any means creative – who insist on stirring the pudding and adding ingredients of their own, I said: 'Very few films qualify as works of art because films are made by committees and committees don't produce art.'

'Yeah?' he said. 'What about cathedrals?'

Right. Well. Cathedrals – yes, not at all a bad point and suddenly this seemed an opportune moment to change the subject. But now flash forward to 1991 when we met again at Cannes where *Homicide*, Mamet's third film as a director, was being shown in the festival and he said: 'Do you remember that conversation we had in New York? About films, art and committees? Well, I've changed my mind. I think you were right.'

I didn't like to ask him what kind of trouble he had had with film-making committees (producers, studios, financial backers and the like) in the interim; it was obviously too painful a subject. But those experiences had clearly left their mark and, though I'm not saying that because he had come round to my way of thinking he was a wiser man, he was certainly a less optimistic one.

For another opinion on much the same subject let me cite Robert Altman, whom I interviewed some while ago for an article in *The Times* and what he said was this: 'I don't think a really good film has been made yet. We're still too closely connected with literature and the theatre. I think the true art of film will be discovered by some kid who's probably out riding his bicycle right now. When it's finally discovered I sense that it will have the effect of making an audience leave the theatre impressed and overwhelmed and yet unable to articulate what it has seen, because the picture will have worked on so many senses at the same time. I'm looking, we're all looking, for that art but I don't quite know what I'm looking for except that I feel that language is now getting away from just words and into every other form of communication.'

By that austere token, of course, no good film has been made to this day and the kid who will finally discover the art is probably still out riding his bicycle. By and large audiences can always leave the cinema easily able to articulate what they have seen, although many films have occasional scenes which do measure up to Altman's ideal. The opening sequence in Alan Parker's *Mississippi Burning* is an example. The nighttime pursuit of three terrified young civil rights workers by a whole cavalcade of murderous bigots intent on killing them was pure cinema. No other medium, not the theatre and not even film's first cousin, television, could have depicted it so vividly; no writer could have conveyed with such power the atmosphere, the tension, the fear, the unspoken certainty that something truly dreadful was about to happen. *Mississippi Burning* is a fine picture but nothing in the rest of it can compare with the opening scenes.

However, I don't think we should take Altman's definition too seriously because what he is looking for is perfection. Perhaps, though, we could go back to David Mamet's original riposte and think of great films as the cinematic equivalents of cathedrals in which the work and skills of artists and artisans alike have blended magically together.

With that analogy in mind how did I choose my own 100 cathedrals? Well, for a start it took the best part of six months of viewing, reviewing, reading and general agonising. I suppose I could have made life easier for myself by consulting other people's lists but that would have been cheating. A catalogue or inventory drawn up by consensus is, in effect, merely the work of another committee; it allows little room for personal taste or idiosyncrasy and in any event has no greater claim than any other list to be regarded as definitive.

In the first edition of this book I wrote: 'What follows then is a compilation of films which I admire and/or like...The one criterion which, I submit, they all satisfy is that they have legs, marathon runners' legs: they have stood the test of time. And because I have applied that test I have not included many films of the last decade or so for their staying power has yet to be proven.'

That last sentence, I now believe, was over-cautious, though it seemed justified at the time. For I then went on to speculate about the possibility of greatness being conferred later upon films which I had not included in my 100 – among them Costner's *Dances With Wolves*, Brian De Palma's *The Untouchables*, Sergio Leone's *Once Upon a Time in America*, Oliver Stone's *Salvador*, *Mephisto* with its superb performance by Klaus Maria Brandauer, and Scorsese's *Cape Fear*. The latter, I predicted, would one day be recognised as a classic. Today I don't think so and of the others I suspect only *Once Upon a Time in America,* despite, or perhaps because of, its inscrutable ending, might one day qualify in any future list I drew up.

The most recent film in the original edition was *Hannah and Her Sisters,* made in 1986. Over-cautious again? No, not really, for while revising this book it struck me that for several years after 1986 no great, or potentially great, film was made. The 1990s, however, have already produced a rich crop of pictures which, ignoring my own original, careful guidelines, I have no hesitation in including here because I am already sure that they will appear in other lists of the 100 best for years to come.

Which are they? In no sort of order of merit they are *Unforgiven,* *Schindler's List, Pulp Fiction* and – cheating a little – Kieslowski's *Three Colours* ... trilogy. No *Titanic?* Certainly not, though it would demand a place in any list of the most over-praised films of the century. One that came very close to forcing its way in was Curtis Hanson's *L.A. Confidential,* a brilliant thriller that was shamefully neglected in both the American and British academy awards of 1998. But – and maybe this is caution intruding again – I think it needs a little more time to mature.

As to the films I left out to accommodate the newcomers – D. W. Griffith's *Birth of a Nation,* Sam Peckinpah's *The Wild Bunch,* Sidney Lumet's *Dog Day Afternoon* and Jean Cocteau's *Orpheus* – all I can do is offer them sincere apologies. They have not, in a few years, become less great films; it is simply that right now, and after much agonising, I prefer their replacements – all of which, I realise, were made, coincidentally and for the purposes of this book happily, in the first hundred years of the cinema. So what you have here is, far more than the original edition, my definitive choice.

To revise a list is obviously easier than to draw it up in the first place. Back in 1992 when I first undertook the task I began with a selection which slowly became shorter, then shorter still until it took its final, arbitrary shape. And when I looked through it what surprised me was not the films I had chosen but those I had omitted. Among the first titles I had jotted down for inclusion was Fellini's *La Dolce Vita* but, on re-viewing, it was a great disappointment: a classic movie for its time but now too dated to be a great movie for all time. François Truffaut's *Jules et Jim* fits into the same category – dazzling at first sight, far less impressive thirty years later. Then, too, there are such works as Friedrich Murnau's *Nosferatu* or Carl Dreyer's *The Passion of Joan of Arc,* both regarded by many purists as seminal. But are they really? Quite apart from the fact that there are very few opportunities to see them these days I wonder how much impact they would have on a modern audience. Have they not perhaps become simply films which scholars like to pore over?

In a different bracket come such pictures as Ingmar Bergman's *Fanny and Alexander,* which, marvellous though it is, still shows signs of having been edited down from the longer TV version, and the same director's *Cries and Whispers*, a powerful piece of cinema which I admire enormously but which I simply cannot bring myself to like. I'm extremely glad to have seen it but nothing would induce me to watch it again. I have much the same reaction to Woody Allen's terminally glum *Interiors*, which many people put among his best works. Personally I never thought it was even a very good film because it seemed to me to be nothing more than ersatz Bergman. But, since we're talking of Woody Allen, why you may wonder no *Annie Hall* or *Manhattan*? Because much as I like them I'm not convinced that they will endure in the way that his earlier, simpler comedies will.

Oh, there are many glaring omissions here to be sure, so many films that didn't quite make the final list: Fellini's *8½* among them as well as Welles's *The Chimes at Midnight*, which, according to your point of view is either rubbish or a near-masterpiece, Jean-Paul Rappeneau's *Cyrano de Bergerac* with the masterly Gérard Depardieu, or even Alan J. Pakula's *Klute*, which is raised above the level of a first-rate thriller by a superb performance from Jane Fonda. Many will deplore their absence and that of many more; others will applaud it. But the fact that such pictures are not included does not mean that I don't admire or like them. It just means that there are other works by other people that I prefer. In the end personal prejudice is inseparable from a selection such as this. Woody Allen is a case in point. Some people can't abide him; I think he's one of the outstanding talents of contemporary cinema. If Chaplin was a genius, then so is Allen. And what's more Allen is much funnier. Also westerns: I have a penchant for them, others don't. Westerns even more than musicals are America's outstanding contribution to the cinema; the best of them are not just exciting adventure stories but modern morality plays. Until Clint Eastwood made *Unforgiven* the last classic addition to this now, alas, generally moribund genre was *The Outlaw Josey Wales*, also made by Eastwood; it is not, however, included here because although it is a great western the competition for space was simply too strong for it.

Nor, after a great deal of thought, did I find room for *The Cruel Sea*.

The acting style looks very dated nowadays but it is still, I submit, a classic British war picture, which, nearly forty years after it was made, regularly attracts large audiences whenever it is shown on TV. I left it out for one reason only: it was produced by my father, Leslie Norman, and proud as I am of his work I do not wish to be accused of some kind of nepotism.

You will, incidentally, notice that a lot of the films mentioned here are American. I feel no need to apologise for that. It's fashionable to sneer at American, and especially Hollywood, films because as I said in the previous chapter, the bulk of the output from there is determinedly populist. In America the cinema has always been an industry; a movie there is 'a product', as it might be a can of baked beans. Thus there is always plenty of ammunition for those who deride Hollywood and insist that the target it aims at has 'lowest common denominator' scrawled across the bull's-eye. Often that is true, but at their best American film makers are as good as any, and the fact that they regard movies as primarily entertainment does not mean that they cannot produce art. Shakespeare regarded the theatre as entertainment, as a way of making a living, but you'd have to be wilfully perverse to deny that he was an artist. Entertainment is not a dirty word. The greatest writers and, come to that, the greatest film makers were quick to realise that the most serious message will fall upon more receptive ears if it is entertainingly presented. That is why movies are nearly always at their best, most effective and most artistic when they are not consciously and solemnly striving to be art.

British films, too, are quite strongly represented here, more strongly indeed than I had thought they would be when I began. Over the decades Britain has produced some exceptionally fine movies and surprisingly continues to turn out a handful of very good ones every year despite the financially straitened circumstances of the industry and the general absence nowadays of specialist screen writers in the tradition of T.E.B. Clarke, William Rose, the Boulting Brothers and Frank Launder and Sidney Gilliat. Very often in the present era scripts are written by novelists and playwrights who seem (though this may be unfair to them) to regard films as a lucrative sideline, interesting no doubt but not to be taken as seriously as the day job. They bring to the cinema a polished literary quality but rarely the visual flair or excitement that are virtually the small change of even so-so Hollywood pictures. In truth, intellectual snobbery still surrounds the cinema in Britain; we do not really cherish it or consider it as serious. A novelist who wins the Booker Prize, no matter how few people actually buy or read his or her book, is held in far greater esteem than, say, a Colin Welland who wins an Oscar for the screenplay of *Chariots of Fire*. In America this would not be so. There film writing is accepted as an honourable trade, different from but not inferior to the writing of novels or stage plays. Here, and despite the fact that each has produced a number of first-rate screenplays, Harold Pinter and Tom Stoppard, for example, are invariably described as playwrights; in America William Goldman, a prolific and successful novelist, is nevertheless far better known for having written the likes of *Butch Cassidy and the Sundance Kid* and *All the President's Men*, for both of which, incidentally, he won Oscars. It's a difference of attitude; Robert Altman was speaking generally when he said that films were still too closely connected with literature and the theatre but his remark applies to the British cinema in particular.

On that subject of Oscars you will see that those are the only awards and nominations that I have listed. I have not mentioned the prizes films won at Cannes, Venice or other international festivals. To do so would have taken up too much space and besides as far as most cinemagoers, and even film makers, are concerned they are of less significance. A few years ago David Puttnam told me that winning the Palme d'Or at Cannes made comparatively little difference to a film's box-office take in Europe and none at all in America. Indeed, he said, such an award could actually work against a picture in the USA where it might consequently be perceived as 'arty'. This is probably less true now that more American companies are allowing their films to be entered in competition in the European festivals, but the fact remains that the Oscar is the one prize above all that every film maker wants and that every cinemagoer remembers.

Dedicated cineastes will no doubt disagree, but in truth the Oscars are not always as crass as they are often made out to be. Sometimes the American Academy does get it right, although to be sure it is equally capable of getting it wildly wrong. (But then so, too, are Cannes, Venice, Berlin and the others; glittering prizes have been heaped upon some very bizarre movies even at the best of festivals.)

When the Oscar voters do get it wrong it's often because of their desire to be seen as serious men and women of the cinema. That's why comedies hardly ever win. A good comedy is harder to make than a good drama but comedy is looked upon as frivolous. Then, too, the voters are much inclined to be swayed by the size and 'importance' of a film. Thus the admirable but conventional *Gandhi* wins out over *E.T.*, which is full of cinematic magic and invention – the very qualities which the voters, themselves employed in the industry, should have prized and rewarded. In addition the voters are shy of films which seem to rock the boat and, if given the choice, will usually go for something safe – *Gone with the Wind* rather than *Citizen Kane*; *Kramer vs. Kramer* rather than *Apocalypse Now*.

On reflection, perhaps, where the Academy most often gets it right is in the nomination stage rather than in the final result, which lends strength to the argument that maybe there should be no final stage, that the whole thing should end with the nominations before the electorate has a chance to lose its bottle and go for the safe option. Most of the American films in my list (westerns and comedies apart) have at least been nominated even though the proportion of them that went on to win may not be particularly high.

But enough. What follows now is my choice of the 100 best films of the first century of the cinema. Not even for me, still less for you, is it engraved on tablets of stone or preserved in aspic. Some while ago an American magazine asked a number of prominent movie people to name their ten most indispensable films. All of them finally, and after deep thought, arrived at ten; but Martin Scorsese had to be begged to stop when he had reached 125. I have much sympathy with him. To be required to choose 100 from 232,000 films – or whatever proportion of them one has seen – is a hugely difficult task. The choice you make – upbeat or downbeat – could depend on something as variable as the mood you are in when you make it or as susceptible to change as the circumstances of your own life at the particular time. In any event if, ten years from now, I were to revise this book the list would certainly be different, perhaps substantially so. Like everything else the cinema has its vintage and its nonvintage years but there is a constant flow, sometimes admittedly dwindling to a trickle, of potential classics. Films take time to mature and some which will eventually come to be regarded as great are undoubtedly maturing even now. What I would claim here, however, is that, for the moment, I will settle happily for this lot. Leave me on a desert island with a big screen, a good projector and pristine prints of these pictures and it would be some time before any thought of escape entered my mind.

The Films

The Adventures Of Robin Hood (1938)

The legend of Robin Hood has been explored many times and in many forms both for the cinema and television but this is the definitive version, probably the most delightful and most satisfying of all adventure movies. It established Errol Flynn as the quintessential swashbuckler, better even than Douglas Fairbanks, sen., who rarely had the additional burden of dialogue to deal with. Flynn was an actor of only limited range but he was a *great* Robin Hood because he brought conviction to the role. A touch of self-mockery, too, of course, but his was the winning and necessary self-mockery of a man who simply knew he was a hero and could therefore afford to take the mickey out of himself. Without that humour he might have been too perfect to be likeable. Conviction, though, was the keynote of the film. Everyone, from Flynn to the Merry Men, from Olivia de Havilland as the delectable Maid Marian to the two magnificent villains, Basil Rathbone as Sir Guy of Gisbourne and Claude Rains as Prince John, behaved as though he or she believed implicitly in the story that was unfolding. A script that blended drama, romance, action and just enough comedy and wit to maintain a perfect rhythm, an England convincingly reconstructed in California and the early use of three-colour Technicolor helped greatly in creating the overall effect. So, especially, did the direction, which is credited to Michael Curtiz and William Keighley. Keighley, who made such films as *G Men* and *Each Dawn I Die*, was a good journeyman; Curtiz, direc-

tor of *Yankee Doodle Dandy* and, of course, *Casablanca*, was much more than that, and in the pace and vivacity of the film it was clearly his influence that prevailed. Yet some credit for the excellence of the picture should also be given to the often-maligned 'studio system'. The 1991 *Robin Hood: Prince of Thieves*, starring Kevin Costner, was fatally flawed by the fact that the villainous Sheriff of Nottingham (Alan Rickman) was written, and therefore played, as a kind of sadistic buffoon. Cynically, one suspects that this was to ensure that the star should not be overshadowed or even rivalled by an even better actor. In 1938 when the studios (in this case Warner Brothers) were all-powerful, stars were not accorded such protection: the balance of the story demanded that Robin should confront adversaries cruel and menacing enough to be worthy of him. And Flynn, rising superbly to the challenge provided by Rathbone and Rains, gave the finest performance of his career.

MAIN CAST: Errol Flynn, Olivia de Havilland, Basil Rathbone, Claude Rains, Alan Hale, Eugene Pallette, Patric Knowles, Ian Hunter. DIR: Michael Curtiz and William Keighley; PROD: Hal B. Wallis; SCR: Seton I. Miller, Norman Reilly Raine; PHOT: Tony Gaudio, Sol Polito, Howard Green; MUS: Erich Wolfgang Korngold.

OSCARS: Best art direction (Carl J. Weyl); best original score; best film editing (Ralph Dawson). OSCAR NOMINATIONS: Best film. (Winner best film 1938: *You Can't Take It with You*.)

106 minutes. Colour

In *Robin Hood: Prince of Thieves* Sean Connery appeared unexpectedly as King Richard. The sublime 1938 version needed no such gimmicks.

The African Queen (1951)

In his novel *White Hunter, Black Heart*, Peter Viertel claims that John Huston insisted on filming *The African Queen* on location in the Congo rather than on the back lot of some studio simply because he wanted to go on safari and, he hoped, shoot an elephant. Knowledge of Huston's character suggests that this is very probably true. Whether it is or not, to film on location was an inspired decision which, with the unconventional but equally inspired casting of Humphrey Bogart and Katharine Hepburn, made *The African Queen* an exceptional movie. Bogart as an ignorant, gin-soaked riverboat captain; Hepburn as a dried-up spinster, a prim, forbidding English missionary? No, no, you think, only Hollywood could have come up with anything so preposterous. And yet it works. As we watch this unlikely couple fleeing from the German forces in the First World War, making their hazardous way down a barely navigable river, taking Bogart's boat, *The African Queen*, through perilous rapids while at first despising each other, then gradually, reluctantly, falling in love, disbelief virtually suspends itself. No effort is required because the

splendour – and obvious discomfort – of the locations is clearly genuine and because these people, changing and growing, discovering within themselves and each other qualities of strength and resourcefulness that neither had suspected, are eminently credible. There is romance here, danger, excitement and a leavening humour that springs naturally from the characters and the situations. Admittedly the climax, the daring assault on the German cruiser, is sentimental, glib and – let's be honest – highly implausible. But above all it is *right*. Nothing less than a triumphant ending would have been remotely acceptable. Incidentally, Peter Viertel worked, uncredited, on the script. His book, one of the best novels about the movie industry, was filmed in 1990 with Clint Eastwood as the thinly disguised Huston. Both on page and on screen it makes an interesting companion piece to *The African Queen* itself.

MAIN CAST: Humphrey Bogart, Katharine Hepburn, Robert Morley, Peter Bull, Theodore Bikel. DIR: John Huston; prod: Sam Spiegel; SCR: James Agee and Huston (from the novel by C.S. Forester); PHOT: Jack Cardiff; MUS: Allan Gray.

OSCAR: Best actor (Bogart). OSCAR NOMINATIONS: Best actress (Hepburn); best director; best screenplay. (Winner best film 1951: *An American in Paris*.)

103 minutes. Colour

John Huston's 'feelings of special tenderness' for the *African Queen* are hardly shared here by Bogart and Hepburn.

All About Eve (1950)

The basic story is high-quality corn – a great, but fading, Broadway star (Bette Davis) is threatened by a sugary sweet, ruthlessly unscrupulous young actress (Anne Baxter), who worms her way into the older woman's life and then plots to replace her both in the theatre and in bed. This is the stuff of traditional backstage drama, but the film soars way above that level thanks to a glittering performance from Davis, an immaculate supporting cast and, most of all, the savage and devastating wit of Joseph L. Mankiewicz's script.

Mankiewicz, one of the most literate, civilised and very probably cynical men ever to work in Hollywood, was at the height of his career. The previous year he had won Oscars for both direction and screenplay for *A Letter to Three Wives*; uniquely, he was to repeat that double with *All About Eve*. The film has been criticised as 'ersatz art' (whatever that may be) and for its 'bad taste'. But, as Mel Brooks has proved in his own best movies, bad taste can be glorious and here it is deliberate, funny, designed to shock and anyway

forgivable in a film in which every line is worth listening to and many (such as Davis's 'Fasten your seat belts, it's going to be a bumpy night') are memorable. George Sanders is splendid as the waspishly malicious drama critic, Thelma Ritter equally so as Davis's dresser, and Marilyn Monroe makes a brief but eye-catching appearance as 'a graduate of the Copacabana School of Dramatic Arts'. (The picture was inspired by Mary Orr's short story, 'The Wisdom of Eve'.)

The protagonists – Bette Davis (left), who has everything, and Anne Baxter (centre below), who plots to take it from her.

MAIN CAST: Bette Davis, George Sanders, Anne Baxter, Celeste Holm, Thelma Ritter, Gary Merrill, Hugh Marlowe. DIR/SCR: Joseph L. Mankiewicz; PROD: Darryl F. Zanuck; PHOT: Milton Krasner; MUS: Alfred Newman.

OSCARS: Best film; best director; best screenplay; best supporting actor (Sanders); best black-and-white costume design (Edith Head, Charles LeMaire); best sound recording (20th Century Fox sound department). OSCAR NOMINATIONS: Best actress (Davis and Baxter); best supporting actress (Holm and Ritter); best cinematography; best art direction/set decoration (Lyle Wheeler, George Davis, Thomas Little, Walter M. Scott); best music; best film editing (Barbara McLean).

138 minutes. B&W

All Quiet On The Western Front (1930)

This was the first great antiwar film (indeed the first classic film) of the sound era, remarkable both for its pacifist message and for the fact that it dealt not with 'our boys' but with the enemy. The story, adapted from Erich Maria Remarque's bestselling novel, deals with a group of young German volunteers in the Great War. When we first meet them they are schoolboys – optimistic, patriotic, imbued with belief in the glory of the fatherland. But then, as they face the grotesque squalor of life in the trenches and begin to comprehend the enormity and the senseless waste of war, their romantic illusions are swiftly shattered, their idealism is eroded. The final shot, of a soldier reaching out to touch a butterfly only a second before he is mortally wounded by an enemy bullet, still provides one of the most vivid and unforgettable moments in all cinema. Among the many strengths of the film (which, incidentally, has often been banned in countries preparing for military action) is that it makes no concession to public demand for a happy ending; nor should it, for ultimately war has no happy ending. It was a brave subject for Hollywood to tackle at the time when the Depression was beginning to hurt and audiences were looking for escapism. Yet it was a great success, perhaps because technically it was astonishing for its time. In this new age of talkies, when equipment was still primitive, the director, Lewis Milestone, was one of the first to use a giant crane to obtain a panoramic sweep of the muddy, churned-up landscape in which men were fighting and dying. The result is a realistic view of trench warfare that has been equalled only in Stanley Kubrick's 1957 *Paths of Glory*. The nominal star was Lew Ayres, who, the previous year, had co-starred with Garbo in her last silent picture, *The Kiss*. He was only 21 at the time, but though he went on to a long and successful career that faded somewhat when (coincidentally or not) he declared himself a conscientious objector in the Second World War, *All Quiet* is the film for which he will be best remembered. Much the same might be said of Milestone, the true star of the picture. Although he directed many other fine movies, among them the 1931 version of *The Front Page*, *All Quiet on the Western Front* remains his masterpiece.

MAIN CAST: Lew Ayres, Louis Wolheim, Slim Summerville, John Wray, Raymond Griffith. DIR: Lewis Milestone; PROD: Carl Laemmle, jun.; SCR: Milestone, Maxwell Anderson, Del Andrews, George Abbott (from the novel by Erich Maria Remarque); PHOT: Arthur Edeson; MUS: David Broekman.

OSCARS: Best film; best director. OSCAR NOMINATIONS: Best screenplay; best cinematography.

140 minutes. B&W

Lew Ayres: idealism has gone. Now only despair, defeat and death await.

Apocalypse Now (1979)

What we have here is a great, sprawling, deeply flawed, pretentious, self-indulgent and yet, in the end, magnificent picture. When Francis Coppola showed it as a work in progress at the Cannes Film Festival he said it was 'more of an experience than a movie' and that just about sums it up. Ostensibly, of course, it's about the Vietnam War, about US Army captain Martin Sheen's progress through the jungle, the skirmishes and the battlefields on a mission to assassinate Marlon Brando's mad and dangerous Colonel Kurtz, a maverick soldier who had become a kind of demigod. But, starting out as a modern parallel to Joseph Conrad's *Heart of Darkness*, the film proceeds to encompass all manner of psychology and myth (death and regeneration, for example) to become both a nightmare journey through the horror and madness of war and an examination of the evil rooted in men's souls. What remains in the mind is not so much the story – as Coppola has said, that becomes less important as the film goes on – as a series of astonishing vignettes: Robert Duvall as a crazy, water-skiing commander; helicopter gunships going into action to the accompaniment of 'The Ride of the Valkyries'; the huge, gross appearance of Brando, half in light, half in darkness. By all accounts the filming (in the Philippines) was a horrendous experience: the budget soared from $12 million to more than $30 million; Martin Sheen had a massive heart attack; and the picture went so far over schedule that in Hollywood it was known as 'Apocalypse Later'. Somehow one feels that what Coppola set out to shoot was not the film he finally delivered, but no matter. For all its faults *Apocalypse Now* is still by far the best of all the Vietnam movies and a riveting condemnation of the appalling damage war can do to people, psychologically as well as physically.

'You have a right to kill me ... but you have no right to judge me.' – Brando to his nemesis, Martin Sheen.

MAIN CAST: Martin Sheen, Robert Duvall, Marlon Brando, Frederic Forrest, Dennis Hopper, Sam Bottoms. DIR/PROD: Francis Coppola; SCR: Coppola, John Milius; phot: Vittorio Storaro; MUS: Carmine Coppola, Francis Coppola.

OSCARS: Best cinematography; best sound recording (Walter Murch, Mark Berger, Richard Beggs, Nat Boxer). OSCAR NOMINATIONS: Best film; best director; best screenplay; best supporting actor (Duvall); best art direction/set decoration (Dean Tavoularis, Angelo Graham, George R. Nelson); best film editing (Richard Marks, Walter Murch, Gerald B. Greenberg, Lis Fruchtman). (Winner best film 1979: *Kramer vs. Kramer*.)

153 minutes. Colour

Bad Day at Black Rock (1955)

From the title you might think it was a western and in a way that's what it is – a modern western, set in a tiny desert town in the American southwest soon after the Second World War. For Black Rock the bad day begins when a train pulls into town and a one-armed stranger (Spencer Tracy) steps down and begins to ask awkward questions. To him, though, the questions do not initially seem awkward at all. He has merely come to give a local Japanese-American farmer the medal awarded posthumously to his soldier son. But the townspeople, led by the ever-menacing Robert Ryan, close ranks against the stranger and as the heat of the day increases, so does the tension. Something quite dreadful has obviously happened here and it's up to Tracy, alone, to discover what it was. This is very high-class melodrama. The basic situation – the stranger (albeit usually with both arms intact) riding into a hostile town – has been used many times since, though rarely as well. *Bad Day at Black Rock* is superior to others of its kind because not a word, a glance nor an action is wasted, either in the script or direction. It's a taut, spare, economical film which yet has the confidence to take its time. We know that violence is about to erupt but we have to wait for it, and wait for it, so that when finally it comes it is infinitely more shocking than any number of contemporary stabbings, shootings and general bloodbaths. The superb technical craftsmanship is equalled by the performances – Tracy immaculate as ever, Ryan at his best and a first-rate supporting cast. But

Bad Day at Black Rock is more than merely a splendidly made, well-acted mystery/thriller. It also deals with a serious social issue – the outrageous treatment of Japanese-Americans in the USA during the Second World War. This was more closely studied in Alan Parker's 1990 *Come See the Paradise*; but *Bad Day at Black Rock* was, commendably, the first Hollywood film even to mention the matter.

MAIN CAST: Spencer Tracy, Robert Ryan, Dean Jagger, Ernest Borgnine, Walter Brennan, Lee Marvin, Anne Francis. DIR: John Sturges; PROD: Dore Schary; SCR: Millard Kaufman (from the story 'Bad Day at Hondo' by Howard Briskin); PHOT: William C. Mellor; MUS: André Previn.

OSCAR NOMINATIONS: Best actor (Tracy); best director; best screenplay. (Winner best film 1955: *Marty*.)

81 minutes. Colour

Horsepower instead of horses, a suitcase instead of a saddlebag – but still the classic western confrontation.

Bambi (1942)

I guarantee that nobody who has seen this film will ever forget the death of Bambi's mother. It has caused copious tears and almost unbearable grief in generations of small children for fifty years as well as providing them with one of the most memorable movie moments of their lives, comparable to that awful time when we just *know* that E.T. is dead. Brave of Disney, really, to include such a scene, though a pretty harsh way to make young people aware that life is real, life is earnest and anyway doesn't last for ever. On the other hand it's a nice antidote to the sentimentality which here, as in all Disney's cartoons, permeates much of the story – the story of Bambi's life from birth to happy ending when he and Faline, the long-lashed doe, go off together into (as one explains to the children) the deer's equivalent of wedlock. The animation, as one expected from all the earlier Disney cartoons, is spectacularly good, the young hero is very appealing, there's menace provided by the dastardly human hunters and a terrifying forest fire and there's a splendid comic scene-stealer in Thumper, the rabbit, who must rank high in everyone's list of favourite cartoon characters. The sentimentality is undoubtedly a touch gooey at times, but woven into it is quite a serious message about birth, life, death and the struggle to survive in a tough old world. Children will probably ignore all that stuff but it's there if they want it and that solemn undertone lends *Bambi* (a remarkable achievement in any case) a significance that is most unusual in an animated feature.

SUPERVISING DIRECTOR: David Hand; STORY DIRECTOR: Perce Pearce; MUS: Frank Churchill, Edward Plumb.

OSCAR NOMINATIONS: Best song ('Love is a Song', mus by Frank Churchill, lyr by Larry Morey); best score; best sound recording (Sam Slyfield). (Winner best film 1942: *Mrs Miniver*.)

69.5 minutes. Colour

The newborn Bambi, the inquisitive Bambi (and, of course, Thumper) in the blissful time before he became an orphan.

The Bank Dick (1940)

In his biography of W.C. Fields, Robert Lewis Taylor describes *The Bank Dick* as 'One of the great classics of American comedy.' So it is. And yet on the face of it the film is a total nonsense – a tottering edifice of implausibility laid precariously upon improbability if not impossibility. Consider: in Lompoc, California, the town ne'er-do-well (Fields) inadvertently foils a bank robbery, becomes a local hero, is given the job of bank detective, acquires the deeds to a seemingly worthless mine, drinks (a lot) in the Black Pussy Café, interferes in a low-budget movie production and marries his daughter to her gormless suitor. The whole thing then climaxes in a wild car chase. What is there in this rickety, ramshackle mess to make it a classic comedy? The answer, of course, is W.C. Fields. No other actor could have played it; quite likely no other actor would have wanted to. Fields wrote the script himself under the pseudonym Mahatma Kane Jeeves (although at one point he gave serious consideration to calling himself A. Pismo Clam) and geared it precisely to his own unique mysogynistic, misanthropic, gloriously unsentimental screen persona. He was the greatest of film comedians, a man born years before his time, so different from his contemporaries, and indeed his successors, that there has never been another like him: aggressively defensive, deeply suspicious of his fellow men (and, even more, of women), glumly convinced that any moment now fate would deliver him another frightful blow, but always resilient enough to fight back and with a magnificently healthy dis-

dain of pathos. His personal creed seems to be perfectly summed up in the title of his next film, *Never Give a Sucker an Even Break*. To see him lurching through *The Bank Dick* in that curiously delicate, fastidious way,

sometimes apparently (and quite possibly actually) under the influence of alcohol and, as Kenneth Tynan once wrote, looking and sounding like a cement mixer, is to watch an artist at the top of his form.

A ramshackle plot mixed together – and held together – by a cement mixer of a comedian.

MAIN CAST: W. C. Fields, Franklin Pangborn, Shemp Howard, Jack Norton, Grady Sutton, Cora Witherspoon. DIR: Eddie Cline; PROD: Jack Gross; SCR: Fields (as Mahatma Kane Jeeves); PHOT: Milton Krasner; MUS: Charles Previn.

OSCAR NOMINATIONS: None. (Winner best film 1940: *Rebecca*.)

74 minutes. B&W

The Battleship Potemkin
Bronenosets Potemkin (1925)

There are those who claim that this is the greatest film ever made and granted its continuing influence on the cinema there is much to be said for that argument. Certainly its most striking scene – the massacre of civilians by Tsarist troops on the Odessa Steps – has been imitated, though never equalled, countless times (most recently perhaps in Brian De Palma's 1987 *The Untouchables*) and is without doubt the most famous single sequence in movie history. The picture came about because Eisenstein was commissioned to make a film commemorating the twentieth anniversary of the 1905 revolution. The subject he chose was the mutiny of the sailors on the battleship *Potemkin*, and the subsequent slaugh-

ter of the townspeople who supported them, in the seaport of Odessa. The result was a peerless blend of propaganda and art. Given the conditions in which the film was made (under the watchful eye of the Bolshevik authorities) and its blatant revolutionary zeal, the political message is, to say the least, dubious. But in all other respects *Potemkin* is an astonishingly powerful work. Eisenstein's innovative and again hugely influential use of montage – for example, the stone lions apparently rearing up in support of the people – and rhythmic editing gave it the look of a documentary (which it wasn't) and the feel and excitement of fiction (which, though obviously based on fact, it was). Most films, even some of

the great ones, have an inherent sell-by date; a shelf life that sooner or later (in the case of the great ones, later) come to an end. This is not true of *Potemkin*. Miraculously, it retains a freshness that makes it a new experience each time you see it.

MAIN CAST: A. Antonov, Vladimir Barski, Grigori Alexandrov, M. Gomorov. DIR/SCR: Sergei Eisenstein; PHOT: Edouard Tissé. (The music, incorporated in most modern prints, was written as an accompanying score by Edmund Meisel.)

86 minutes. B&W. Silent

The aftermath of slaughter on the Odessa Steps (opposite) – possibly the most vivid, most imitated image in the cinema.

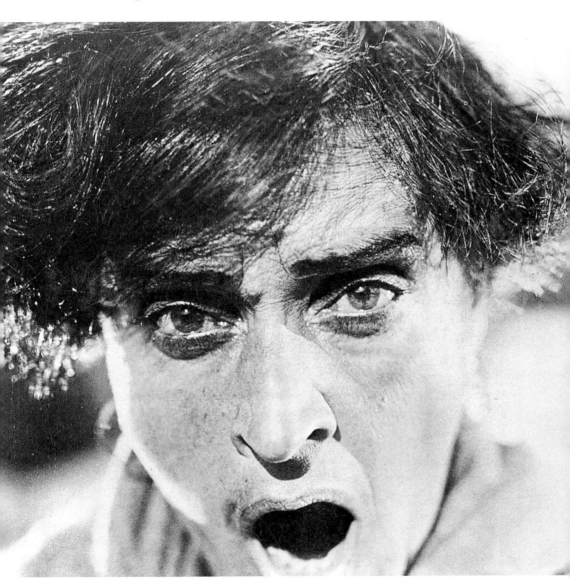

The Best Years Of Our Lives (1946)

Russell and March, Andrews and Mayo in what is still the best film about the social aftermath of war.

Considering the year it was made and Hollywood's general and lamentable propensity to go over the top, this is a surprisingly restrained account of the tribulations facing American servicemen on their return from war. The homecoming warriors (Fredric March, Dana Andrews and Harold Russell) may have been heroes on the battlefield but in their own small town they're just ordinary Joes who, if anything, have fallen behind in the struggle to make a success of civilian life. So there is precious little jingoism here and not much sentimentality either. There are tears, yes, and laughter but mostly the tone is matter-of-fact. Army sergeant March,

though lovingly welcomed home by his wife, Myrna Loy, is so restless and dissatisfied back at the bank that he takes to the bottle; Air Force major Andrews, rejected by his flighty spouse, Virginia Mayo, finds himself stacking shelves for a living and turns for consolation to March's daughter, Teresa Wright; seaman Russell (a non-actor, more or less playing himself, who had lost both arms in the war) agonises over whether, thus handicapped, he should inflict himself on his sweetheart, Cathy O'Donnell. There is scope here for mawkishness on a grand scale but somehow, skilfully, the film avoids it. Naturally, everything turns out well (as

in so many cases it failed to do, two decades later, for those returning from the Vietnam War). Perhaps inevitably *Best Years* now has a slightly dated look to it (see earlier references to sell-by date/shelf life) but it is still an extremely moving, well-made film – probably William Wyler's finest achievement – and a decent, honest and unsensational approach to what was at the time a troubling and universal issue: the problems faced by men, who in many cases had known nothing but war, in adapting to the demands of peacetime.

MAIN CAST: Fredric March, Myrna Loy, Dana Andrews, Teresa Wright, Virginia Mayo, Harold Russell, Hoagy Carmichael, Cathy O'Donnell. DIR: William Wyler; PROD: Samuel Goldwyn; SCR: Robert Sherwood (from the verse novel *Glory For Me* by Mackinlay Kantor); PHOT: Gregg Toland; MUS: Hugo Friedhofer.

OSCARS: Best film; best actor (March); best director; best screenplay; best supporting actor (Russell); best music; best film editing (Daniel Mandell). OSCAR NOMINATIONS: Best sound recording (Gordon Sawyer). SPECIAL AWARD: Russell 'for bringing hope and courage to his fellow veterans through his appearance in *The Best Years of Our Lives*.'

182 minutes. B&W

Bicycle Thieves
Ladri di Biciclette (1938)

The cunning use of a small boy lends emotional impact to a story otherwise lacking in sentimentality.

In this deceptively simple story, Vittorio de Sica gives us the very essence of the 1940s Italian school of neorealism, a movement that started as a protest against and a rejection of the glossy, state-sponsored films of the Fascist era. The object of neorealism was, to borrow Hemingway's phrase, 'to tell it like it is'; to make the audience confront the supposedly real world instead of the glossy version normally presented by the movies. Here, classically, de Sica did it by using actual locations and a largely non-professional cast in telling of a long-unemployed bill sticker, who is finally offered a job but can't do it without his bicycle. He redeems the bike from the pawnshop and promptly has it stolen; so he and his small son spend their Sunday fruitlessly searching for it. Nothing could be more basic than that, except that de Sica turns the couple's quest into an urban Odyssey through the poorest quarters of the city and into a bitter cry against poverty and the Establishment (including the Church) that permits it. This could easily have become grim fare but it is never that because of the warmth and sympathy, the gentle romanticism, with which the film is imbued. It could be argued – and I would even argue it myself – that this is not a charming film, one that clasps you emotionally to its bosom; nor does it work (if it was ever intended to be such) as a general meditation on the human condition. But as a piece of social realism, a study of a society in which something as apparently trivial as the theft of a bicycle can be all-important, it is, unquestionably, a great film.

MAIN CAST: Lamberto Maggiorani, Enzo Staiola, Lianella Carell, Gino Saltamarenda. DIR: Vittorio de Sica; PROD: Umberto Scarparelli; SCR: Cesare Zavattini; PHOT: Carlo Montuori; MUS: Alessandro Cicognini.

OSCAR NOMINATION: Best screenplay. SPECIAL AWARD: Outstanding foreign language film. (Winner best film 1949: *All the King's Men*.)

90 minutes. B&W. Italian – subtitled

The Big Sleep (1946)

It's an indisputable fact that for anyone addicted to the works of Raymond Chandler no actor can make a wholly satisfactory Philip Marlowe, since Marlowe is clearly the spitting image of the reader – or, if the reader happens to be female, of her ideal man. But in this gloriously moody, sultry, sexy – to say nothing of incredibly complicated – *film noir*, Humphrey Bogart comes closer than anyone else. Here Marlowe, hired by the invalid General Sternwood to protect his younger daughter (the thumb-sucking Martha Vickers) from her own decadence, is immediately plunged into his familiar, dark world of killers, drug addicts, blackmailers, pornographers, spoiled society women and nymphomaniacs. The plot is so complex that at one stage (and I had this from Howard Hawks himself) director and writers phoned Chandler to ask who killed the chauffeur – and even Chandler didn't know. But such trifles are quite unimportant. What counts are the brooding atmosphere, the witty, incisive dialogue, the rich, rounded characters and, not least, the electrically sexy involvement of Bogart and Lauren Bacall, their verbal exchanges quivering with innuendo. To say that *The Big Sleep* is in a different class from virtually every modern detective thriller (and Michael Winner's 1977 remake didn't come within hailing distance, even with an amplified loud-speaker) is probably unfair. After all, where today could you find a team to equal Hawks, Bogart, the young Bacall and William Faulkner?

MAIN CAST: Humphrey Bogart, Lauren Bacall, John Ridgely, Martha Vickers, Dorothy Malone, Regis Toomey, Elisha Cook, jun.; DIR/PROD: Howard Hawks; SCR: William Faulkner, Leigh Brackett, Jules Furthman (from the novel by Raymond Chandler); PHOT: Sid Hickox; MUS: Max Steiner.

OSCAR NOMINATIONS: None. (Winner best film 1946: *The Best Years of Our Lives*.)

114 minutes. B&W

Seductive young women brandishing sex, men brandishing guns – the occupational hazards of a private eye's trade.

Bonnie And Clyde (1967)

A landmark movie this, one that perfectly caught the changing mood of America in the late 60s. Its chronicle of the life and crimes of Bonnie Parker and Clyde Barrow, a couple of small-time, rural desperadoes of the Depression years, is glamorous, funny, vibrant with youthful energy, exceedingly violent, amoral and rebellious. Bonnie and Clyde, roaming the dust-bowls of the Depression, encouraging a bankrupt farmer to shoot up the house from which he had just been evicted,

epitomise – albeit in a hugely exaggerated way – the spirit of the Vietnam era, the growing opposition to the constrictions of society and the Establishment, the feeling that the system could no longer be changed from within, that it had to be blown away. In *Rebel Without a Cause*, which purported to say much the same thing, James Dean was really just a conformist pretending to be a rebel; Bonnie and Clyde were the genuine article and their obvious delight in their exploits, together with their rejection of any idea of conventional family in favour of their own, self-created family of a small, close gang with no stern authority figure appealed to the predominantly youthful audience. And because they are so attractive and so funny the violence is particularly shocking, causing people to halt in mid-laugh until at the end, when the protagonists, riddled with bullets, jerk about in the dust like rag dolls, there is no laughter at all. *Bonnie and Clyde* is one of those rare films that actually changed the cinema, bringing in its wake a whole wave of movies (*Butch Cassidy and the Sundance Kid*, for instance) in which American values are seen from the outlaws' point of view and, because the outlaws are good-looking and empathetic, are rejected or at least challenged. The film boosted the career of Beatty, and established those of Dunaway, Hackman and Penn,

Dunaway recreating the kind of posed photograph that Bonnie and Clyde sent to the newspapers.

although initially the writers wanted François Truffaut or Jean-Luc Godard to direct. Incidentally, Robert Towne, who was called in to polish the dialogue, changed the character of Clyde from a homosexual to an impotent (although not eventually) heterosexual.

MAIN CAST: Warren Beatty, Faye Dunaway, Gene Hackman, Michael J. Pollard, Estelle Parsons, Gene Wilder. DIR: Arthur Penn; PROD: Beatty; SCR: David Newman, Robert Benton; PHOT: Burnett Guffrey; MUS: Charles Strouse.

OSCARS: Best supporting actress (Parsons); best cinematography. OSCAR NOMINATIONS: Best film; best actor (Beatty); best actress (Dunaway); best director; best screenplay; best supporting actor (Hackman and Pollard); best costume design (Theadora van Runkle). (Winner best film 1967: *In the Heat of the Night*.)

111 minutes. Colour

Breathless
A Bout de Souffle (1959)

This was not the first of the *nouvelle vague* movies (Claude Chabrol's *Le Beau Serge* in 1958 can lay strongest claim to that distinction), but it was the one that announced most firmly that the new wave was here and we'd better pay attention. In form it's not much more than an old-fashioned chase story. The feckless, amoral young protagonist (Jean-Paul Belmondo) steals a car, finds a gun, kills a cop, chases around Paris trying to recover money that is owed to him and plans to escape to Italy with his cool, crop-haired American girl-friend (Jean Seberg). It was the style, not the content, that was startling. Everything was shot on location – café scenes took place in cafés, not in studio mock-ups – with, wherever possible, natural lighting and a hand-held camera. Jump cuts replaced establishing shots; scenes continued past the point where they had told us what we needed to know and simply finished when they finished. There was no attempt at social realism. This was cinema for cinema's sake, a reaction against the literary, arty tradition of French film-making. The inspiration was the American B picture, the hard-boiled gangster movies of such directors as Sam Fuller and Don Siegel. The result was something both familiar and excitingly different, a film that moved as breathlessly fast as its restless antihero and was to have a profound effect on European and American film makers alike. Interestingly, *Breathless* was the result of a collaboration by the three biggest icons of the *nouvelle vague*. It was, without doubt, Godard's film, but François Truffaut suggested the story

and Chabrol acted as technical adviser. In 1983 the American director Jim McBride borrowed the title and the plot (more or less) for a remake starring Richard Gere and Valerie Kaprisky. It was not to be compared with the original. But by then Godard's work, still experimental but becoming ever more inscrutable, was not to be compared with *Breathless* either. Apart from anything else, that film virtually introduced the dazzling Belmondo to international audiences and made everyone forgive Jean Seberg for her disastrous *Joan of Arc* two years earlier.

MAIN CAST: Jean-Paul Belmondo, Jean Seberg, Daniel Boulanger, Jean-Pierre Melville. DIR/SCR: Jean-Luc Godard (from a story by François Truffaut); PROD: Georges de Beauregard; PHOT: Raoul Coutard; MUS: Martial Solal.

OSCAR NOMINATIONS: None. (Winner best film 1959: *Ben-Hur*; winner best foreign language film 1959: *Black Orpheus*.)

90 minutes. B&W. French – subtitled

Godard helped launch the *auteur* theory. Here, aided by Belmondo and Seberg, he puts it memorably into effect.

Bringing Up Baby (1938)

Perhaps the highest compliment I can pay to *Bringing up Baby* is that if P. G. Wodehouse had been born an American he might have written it. Like Wodehouse, the film creates a world of its own, one just recognisable to those of us who live in the other world but far more enchanting and carefree than ours. For a start it's inhabited by Katharine Hepburn, the kind of gloriously eccentric, ravishingly beautiful heiress that every man would cheerfully leave home for. Then, too, there's any world's most handsome palaeontologist, Cary Grant, whose life Hepburn throws into lunatic turmoil. Plus, of course, there's a leopard, Hepburn's pet and the Baby of the title – or rather there are two leopards, one far less cute than Baby, and a dog (also belonging to the disruptive Hepburn) who steals a bone from the dinosaur Grant is so painstakingly reconstructing. Add to that the fact that the entire company ends up in jail and even Wodehouse could not have arranged things better. This is simply a joyous film that gives the impression of having

Hepburn and Grant in a relationship in which, as Grant ruefully declares, 'there haven't been any quiet moments'.

been spun from the finest gossamer rather than constructed. The acting, with Grant seizing a godsent opportunity to hone the slightly querulous, slightly gawky performance that was to become his trademark, is immaculate as, too, are the script and, come to that, the direction of Howard Hawks, who moves everything along with the lightest of touches and exquisite comic timing. (The influence of *Baby* can be clearly seen in Peter Bogdanovich's 1972 *What's Up Doc?*.)

MAIN CAST: Katharine Hepburn, Cary Grant, Charles Ruggles, May Robson, Walter Catlett, Fritz Feld, Barry Fitzgerald. DIR/SCR: Howard Hawks; SCR: Dudley Nichols, Hagar Wilde; PHOT: Russell Metty; MUS: Roy Webb.

OSCAR NOMINATIONS: None. (Winner best film 1938: *You Can't Take It with You*.)

102 minutes. B&W

Butch Cassidy and the Sundance Kid (1969)

This was the first, and the best, of all the modern buddy movies and a nostalgic, loving farewell to the great era of the Wild West, the film that declared lyrically and movingly that 'them days is over'. In its highly romanticised depiction of the last months in the lives of two legendary outlaws it's a kind of *Bonnie and Clyde* (or, rather, Clyde and Clyde) set at the turn of the century. The plot follows Butch (Paul Newman) and Sundance (Robert Redford) and the Hole in the Wall gang as they rob the Union Pacific Express not once but twice, only to be foiled at the second attempt. Now, with a specially recruited posse just a brisk gallop behind, the two protagonists head for the suppos-

edly richer pickings of Bolivia, pausing only to collect Sundance's girlfriend (Katharine Ross) and spend a few days lotus-eating in New York. And in Bolivia they meet their deaths in a hail of bullets, much as Bonnie and Clyde had done, though less graphically. Here again we have a pair of almost impossibly attractive antiheroes – individualists, nonconformists, rebels who look at organised society, shake their heads and say they want no part of it. They do not seek violence; it's imposed upon them. Sundance kills only when there is no alternative and Butch has never killed at all until, ironically, he is forced to do so when lawfully guarding another man's property. Nevertheless,

**'Raindrops Keep Fallin' on my Head':
Newman and Ross (left) and with Redford
(above) – irresistible antiheroes defying
organised society right to that last freeze
frame.**

amorality is once more held up for our
admiration and we do admire it thanks
to the charm of the performances, the
wit of the script, the overall style that
gives a faintly fantastical air to the proceedings and the affectionate bonding
between the two men. 'Keep thinking,
Butch,' says the amused Sundance. 'It's
what you're good at.' And so he is.
Even at the end, besieged by what
appears to be the entire Bolivian army,
Butch is planning yet another new start
in Australia and emboldened by this
idea they leap out, still defiant, to face

their enemies. The freeze frame is perfect. We do not wish to see them die;
that would be unbearable. They exist
for ever in that frozen moment and
besides, who knows, Butch may yet
think of a way to get them out of there.

MAIN CAST: Paul Newman, Robert Redford,
Katharine Ross, Strother Martin, Henry
Jones, Cloris Leachman, Jeff Corey. DIR:
George Roy Hill; PROD: John Foreman; SCR:
William Goldman; PHOT: Conrad Hall; MUS:
Burt Bacharach.

OSCARS: Best screenplay; best cinematography; best song ('Raindrops Keep Fallin' on
my Head', mus by Bacharach, lyr by Hal
David). OSCAR NOMINATIONS: Best film;
best director; best sound (William
Edmundson and David Dockendorf).
(Winner best film 1969: *Midnight Cowboy*.)

112 minutes. Colour

Cabaret (1972)

A glossy decadence, at once appealing and repulsive, hangs over *Cabaret*. It's most evident in the cabaret scenes themselves where the corrupt, sweaty, energetic proceedings are overseen by a leering, evil little doll of a master of ceremonies, superbly played by Joel Grey. But it's there, too, in the main story – the relationship between a young Englishman (Michael York) and an ambitious singer (American in the film, since she's played by Liza Minnelli) and their literal seduction by a German baron (Helmut Griem). Yet this sort of decadence, oozing sexuality, seems almost desirable when set against the background – Berlin in the 1930s with the Nazis in power. What they represent, with their fanatical anti-Semitism (exemplified in the plight of York's Jewish friends, Marisa Berenson and Fritz Wepper) and their casual brutality, is a far greater decadence. *Cabaret*, based mainly on Christopher Isherwood's novel *Goodbye to Berlin*, and partly on John Van Druten's stage adaptation of it, *I Am a Camera*, uses the political framework very well, most chillingly when a beautiful boy in the uniform of the Nazi youth stands up at a boulevard café and sings 'Tomorrow Belongs to Me'. The centrepiece, though, is the cabaret itself where Minnelli sings and Grey manipulates and the grotesque, feverish nature of the festivities reflects the despair of the outsiders in Berlin society, who cannot come to terms with and anyway are not accepted by the monstrous regime that rules their country. It's here and in the cross-cutting between the main narrative, the

brooding Nazi presence and the frenetic gaiety of the cabaret that the film is most alive. Minnelli, in her first singing role on screen, may not look like most people's idea of Isherwood's heroine, Sally Bowles, but she brings the right degree of recklessness and vulnerability to the role. The production values – composition, structure, editing, lighting – are first-rate and the result is a musical which is much more than just a musical.

Joel Grey and friends forgetting, briefly, the greater decadence outside the cabaret.

MAIN CAST: Liza Minnelli, Michael York, Joel Grey, Helmut Griem, Marisa Berenson, Fritz Wepper. DIR: Bob Fosse; PROD: Cy Feuer; SCR: Jay Presson Allen (from *Goodbye to Berlin* by Christopher Isherwood); PHOT: Geoffrey Unsworth; MUS: John Kander; LYR: Fred Ebb; MUS DIR: Ralph Burns.

OSCARS: Best actress (Minnelli); best director; best supporting actor (Grey); best cinematography; best art direction/set decoration (Rolf Zehetbauer, Jurgen Kiebach, Herbert Strabel); best music; best sound (Robert Knudson and David Hildyard); best film editing (David Bretherton). OSCAR NOMINATIONS: Best film; best screenplay. (Winner best film 1972: *The Godfather*.)

128 minutes. Colour

Casablanca (1942)

On the face of it there's no reason why *Casablanca* – probably the most frequently revived movie in the world – should ever have been more than a run-of-the-mill, top-of-the-bill programme filler. It has a plot that is by no means guaranteed to work, as Sydney Pollack's 1990 *Havana* quite disastrously proved. And initially Warner Brothers thought so little of the project that, having offered it to George Raft (whose judgement was so suspect that he turned it down, as he had earlier turned down *The Maltese Falcon*), they relegated it to B-picture status by pen-

cilling in Ronald Reagan and Ann Sheridan for the lead roles. It was the promising first draft script by the Epstein twins – plus the happy, though belated, decision to offer the film to Curtiz, the third director approached – that brought about a change of mind and cast and created the *Casablanca* that the world knows and loves. And we love it for a variety of reasons – the faultless supporting cast, the song ('As Time Goes By', which the composer, Max Steiner, urged Warners to omit), the sparkling dialogue, the chemistry that crackled between Bogart and

Bergman. It's the perfect romantic film, a story of star-crossed lovers in a world in turmoil whose love transcends mere self. If Bogart and Bergman had gone off together in the end, *Casablanca* would not now, I think, hold its special place in the memory. But, of course, they did not go off together; instead, acknowledging that in a time of war the immediate happiness of two individuals mattered no more than a hill of beans, they sacrificed love for duty – and so ensured that their love would last for ever. As Bogart says: 'We'll always have Paris.'

Two classic moments – 'Play it, Sam' (left) and 'Round up the usual suspects.'

MAIN CAST: Humphrey Bogart, Ingrid Bergman, Claude Rains, Paul Henreid, Sydney Greenstreet, Peter Loore, S.Z. Sakall, Conrad Veidt, Dooley Wilson (as Sam). DIR: Michael Curtiz; PROD: Hal Wallis; SCR: Jules Epstein, Philip Epstein, Howard Koch (from the then unproduced play *Everybody Comes to Rick's* by Murray Burnett and Joan Alison); PHOT: Arthur Edeson; MUS: Max Steiner.

OSCARS: Best film; best director; best screenplay. OSCAR NOMINATIONS: Best actor (Bogart); best actress (Bergman); best supporting actor (Rains); best cinematography; best music; best film editing (Owen Marks).

102 minutes. B&W

Chinatown (1974)

Chinatown is a superbly crafted thriller, a late 30s period piece that treats its period with such respect and seriousness that it could almost be of it rather than about it. In form it's in the great tradition of the private eye mystery story – the detective (Jack Nicholson) takes on an apparently straightforward investigation whose strands, deeply and at first sight almost inextricably entangled, finally lead back to even greater crimes, including incest. As in the best *film noir* the characters are never quite what they seem. Nicholson, his nose incongruously bandaged for most of the film after it's been slashed by a vicious punk (Roman Polanski), is a mass of moral ambiguities, as cynical as Philip Marlowe but far more vulnerable; the heroine (Faye Dunaway), beautiful but slightly past her sell-by date, is neither the hurt innocent, nor yet a wicked wrongdoer; the arch-villain (John Huston) oozes power and charm, but beneath the surface there is pathos along with evil. *Chinatown* (the title refers less to the place than the state of mind, a condition of being continually on the wrong foot, that it engenders) is a very superior thriller because it runs wide as well as deep. The plot is both logically and excitingly explored and so, too, are the protagonists and the effect of the action on them. Just as Raymond Chandler's books are not merely thrillers but thoughtful novels, so *Chinatown* is both thriller and character study. There are no absolutes, no good guys and bad guys, just guys (male and female) in all of whom innocence and guilt, good and evil are present in lesser or greater degrees.

MAIN TEXT: Jack Nicholson, Faye Dunaway, John Huston, Perry Lopez, John Hillerman, Diane Ladd. DIR: Roman Polanski; PROD: Robert Evans; SCR: Robert Towne; PHOT: John A. Alonso; MUS: Jerry Goldsmith.

OSCAR: Best screenplay. OSCAR NOMINA-
TIONS: Best film; best actor (Nicholson);
best actress (Dunaway); best director; best
cinematography; best art direction/set deco-
ration (Richard Sylbert, W. Stewart
Campbell, Ruby Levitt); best music; best
costumes (Anthea Sylbert); best sound (Bud
Grenzbach, Larry Jose); best film editing
(Sam O'Steen). (Winner best film 1974: *The
Godfather Part II*.)

113 minutes. Colour

**As Nicholson told the policeman, when
explaining the cut on his nose: 'Your wife
crossed her legs.'**

Citizen Kane (1941)

Another contender (and very likely the one with the strongest claim) for the title of 'the greatest film ever made'. It might easily be the most influential film ever made. Its use, among other things, of broken (i.e. not necessarily chrono-

logical) narrative and deep-focus composition to set the characters precisely within their surroundings caused François Truffaut to declare that 'everything that matters in cinema since 1940 has been influenced by *Citizen Kane*'. The story has a reporter (William Alland) trying to discover the significance of 'Rosebud', the last word uttered by the dying newspaper magnate Charles Foster Kane (Orson Welles). Gradually, by interviewing the people who were closest to him, he charts the tycoon's progress, professional and social, from childhood to the grave and puts together a portrait of the private and public man. Kane and his wife (Dorothy Comingore), whom he tries unsuccessfully to make into an opera singer, were so closely based on William Randolph Hearst and his mistress, Marion Davies, that Hearst and his papers tried to have the film suppressed. RKO finally released it only after Welles threatened them with a law suit unless they did so. Despite the obvious quality and sheer exuberance of the picture, the controversy adversely affected its initial reception and may possibly have tilted the Oscar voters against it. (Or maybe it was Welles's youth and abundant self-confidence that the voters resented.) In any event it was not at first widely seen as the masterpiece it quite clearly is – a picture that was not only more innovative than any since *The Battleship Potemkin*, but one that matures with age and speaks afresh to each succeeding generation.

MAIN CAST: Orson Welles, Joseph Cotten, Dorothy Comingore, Everett Sloane, Ray Collins, Paul Stewart, Agnes Moorehead, Ruth Warrick, George Coulouris, William Alland. DIR/PROD: Orson Welles; SCR: Welles, Herman J. Mankiewicz; PHOT: Gregg Toland; MUS: Bernard Herrmann.

Welles, the boy wonder, who celebrated his twenty-sixth birthday in the month his film opened, pictured here with Joseph Cotten.

OSCAR: Best screenplay. OSCAR NOMINATIONS: Best film; best actor (Welles); best director; best cinematography; best art direction/interior decoration (Perry Ferguson, Van Nest Polglase, Al Fields, Darrell Silvera); best music; best sound recording (John Aalberg); best film editing (Robert Wise). (Winner best film 1941: *How Green Was My Valley*.)

119 minutes. B&W

The Discreet Charm of the Bourgeoisie (1972)

Everyone who knows the man's work has his/her favourite Buñuel; *Belle de Jour* for some, *Viridiana* for others, *The Exterminating Angel* for a great many more. *Discreet Charm* is mine because it's the most joyful of his films. Ferocious, yes, it's that as well, especially towards the end when reality, or anyway Buñuel's reality – terrorism, murder, torture – creep into what has

hitherto appeared to be a deliciously light comedy about a group of highly civilised and decidedly charming people who, for a variety of mysterious reasons (the absence of a host from his home, of tea from the tearooms, the sudden death of a restaurateur), are continually thwarted in their search for a meal. This is the cinema of the absurd, of the surreal; it's elegant, sexy, funny. But in the Buñuel tradition it's also alarming and occasionally savage, swiping away with blistering wit at the upper classes, the Church, military absurdity and, for good measure, South American politics. Beautifully played, too, by a splendid cast among whom (for me) Stéphane Audran stands out because she is here the epitome of the exquisite, desirable Parisienne, the one whom, in romantic myth and fable, all Parisiennes look like but whom, in fact, only Audran does.

MAIN CAST: Fernando Rey, Delphine Seyrig, Stéphane Audran, Jean-Pierre Cassel, Bulle Ogier, Paul Frankeur, Julien Bertheau. DIR: Luis Buñuel; PROD: Serge Silberman; SCR: Buñuel, Jean-Claude Carrière; PHOT: Edmond Richard.

OSCAR: Best foreign language film. OSCAR NOMINATIONS: Best screenplay. (Winner best film 1972: *The Godfather*.)

105 minutes. Colour. French – subtitled

The characters in search of dinner and finding instead Buñuel's food for the imagination – sex, violence, wit, fantasy and surrealism.

Double Indemnity (1944)

Director Billy Wilder and writer Raymond Chandler combined – not always harmoniously, by all accounts, but most effectively – to produce a piece of classic *film noir*. The title refers to the double insurance benefit paid out in case of accidental death. Thus Barbara Stanwyck and her lover, Fred MacMurray (in one of his rare serious roles), murder her husband and plot to make the death look like an accident, only to be foiled by doggedly suspicious investigator Edward G. Robinson. The story is told by MacMurray in flashback, a device that enables him not only to recount what happened but to gain insight into how he had been manipulated by his accom-plice. He believed himself to be the instigator of the crime, the man in charge, but he was not; as so often in *film noir* it was the woman, the beautiful, deadly *femme fatale*, who really pulled the strings. The concept of the hero/villain (MacMurray), with whom you very nearly sympathise, was not exactly new but it was cleverly used; Stanwyck, cool and teasing and flashing long, raunchy legs, was the archetypal desirable slut; and Robinson was on top form. All this plus realistic settings, taut direction and close attention to visual detail made *Double Indemnity* one of the very best of the 1940s thrillers.

As the movie's publicity slogan so aptly put it: 'You can't kiss away a murder!'

MAIN CAST: Barbara Stanwyck, Fred MacMurray, Edward G. Robinson, Tom Powers. DIR: Billy Wilder; PROD: Joseph Sistrom; SCR: Wilder, Raymond Chandler (from the novel by James M. Cain); PHOT: John Seitz; MUS: Miklos Rozsa.

OSCAR NOMINATIONS: Best film; best actress (Stanwyck); best director; best screenplay; best cinematography; best music; best sound recording (Loren Ryder). (Winner best film 1944: *Going My Way*.)

107 minutes. B&W

Duck Soup (1933)

It's too easy now for young filmgoers to look at the Marx Brothers' movies and say: 'So what?' Almost everything they did has been done again since and in some cases done better. But Groucho, Harpo, Chico (and let's not forget Zeppo and Gummo) did it all first; they were the most innovative of the early comedians and, besides, some of their routines (the stateroom scene in *A Night at the Opera*, for instance) simply cannot be improved upon. *Duck Soup*, though, is their masterpiece, a short, crisp hilarious satire (intentional or otherwise and probably not very intentional) on the politics of war and the Ruritanian romances that Hollywood was so fond of after the advent of the talkies. Groucho woos and wins the wealthy Margaret Dumont (most glorious and statuesque of all straightwomen) with his usual rapid-fire insults, becomes Prime Minister of Freedonia and goes to war with the neighbouring state of Sylvania, whose incompetent agents are Chico and Harpo. The lunacy throughout is never less than inspired (especially in the battle scenes) and there's some business with a broken mirror which is as funny as anything the brothers ever did. *Duck Soup* was their last film for Paramount – and the last in which Zeppo appeared. It was a financial flop on its first release and the studio, suffering money problems anyway, allowed the brothers to go to MGM, where, under the close eye of Irving Thalberg, they made their biggest hit, *A Night at the Opera*, which they thought was their best film. They were wrong – *Duck Soup* is.

Margaret Dumont, who began as a singer but achieved celebrity as the butt of Groucho's insults.

MAIN CAST: Groucho, Chico, Harpo and
Zeppo Marx, Margaret Dumont, Louis
Calhern, Edgar Kennedy, Raquel Torres.
DIR: Leo McCarey; SCR: Bert Kalmar,
Harry Ruby, Arthur Sheekman, Nat Perrin;
PHOT: Henry Sharp; MUS/LYR: Kalmar,
Ruby.

OSCAR NOMINATIONS: None. (Winner best
film 1932–3: *Cavalcade*.)

70 minutes. B&W

Les Enfants du Paradis (1945)
Children of Paradise

During the decade from 1936 to 1946, the writer/director team of Marcel Carné and Jacques Prévert were the prime exponents of the 'poetic realism' school of French cinema. The films they made together in that time included *Drôle de Drame*, *Le Quai des Brumes* and *Le Jour Se Lève*. But the pinnacle

Mime artist Jean-Louis Barrault (left) searches for the elusive Arletty, but Maria Casarès hopes his happiness lies with her.

of their achievement was *Les Enfants du Paradis*, which has since become one of the most celebrated of all films. The work of Carné and Prévert was banned during the Nazi occupation of France, but they were allowed to continue working together and, in fact, made *Les Enfants du Paradis* in 1944, although it was not released until after the liberation. It's a lush, sumptuous epic, originally made in two parts to run for 195 minutes, set in the theatrical society of nineteenth-century Paris and based in several cases on historical figures. It tells of the love – or rather the different kinds of love – felt for a young *ingénue* (Arletty) by four different men: an actor, a mime artist, a murderer and an aristocrat. The theme is indeed about love and the various forms it takes. But it's also about life and theatre and how they impinge upon each other and it's

about the nature of dramatic perfor- mance. This is epic melodrama, power- fully emotional, spectacular to look at, superbly played and extraordinary as an evocation of time and place. Arletty's performance as the fiercely independent, much-wooed Garance puts her up there with the great roman- tic heroines of the cinema.

MAIN CAST: Arletty, Jean-Louis Barrault, Pierre Brasseur, Louis Salou, Marcel Herrand, Pierre Renoir, Maria Casarès. DIR: Marcel Carné; PROD: Fred Orain, Raymond Borderic; SCR: Jacques Prévert; PHOT: Roger Hubert; MUS: Maurice Thiriet, Joseph Kosma, G. Mouque.

OSCAR NOMINAITON (1946): Best screen- play. (Winner best film 1946: *The Best Years of Our Lives*.)

188 minutes. B&W. French – subtitled

E.T. – The Extra-Terrestrial (1982)

finds himself he rapidly becomes cute and loveable but at first sight he is, as one critic put it, 'an ugly little bugger'. And that is deliberate, because along with the adventure and (genuine) sentiment, the film contains a warning against bigotry and prejudice: we should not judge others by their appearance or colour or creed but by their character and their behaviour. The message is understated but clear and gives *E.T.* the moral edge that makes it the ideal modern fairy tale.

E.T. is more – much more – than science fiction, a marvel of special effects or a Disneyesque fantasy. It is a perfectly crafted film that depends as much on plot, narrative and character as it does on the vivid imagination that conceived it. Steven Spielberg describes it, rightly, as a love story – the story of a relationship between a small boy (Henry Thomas) and a curious little creature from another planet whose spaceship takes off without him, leaving him abandoned in suburban America. Thomas becomes his best friend, his protector against authoritarian adults whose menace is chillingly conveyed not by guns but by heavy boots, probing torches and great bunches of keys clanking on their belts. *E.T.* is full of magic, innocence and wonder; it is funny, frightening and deeply touching. At its basic level it is a superbly satisfying entertainment which, like all the best stories, appeals to people of any age. And yet it is even more than that. *E.T.* is not an immediately attractive creature; true, as he bumbles through the alien, human world in which he

MAIN CAST: Henry Thomas, Dee Wallace, Peter Coyote, Drew Barrymore, Robert MacNaughton. DIR: Steven Spielberg; PROD: Spielberg/Kathleen Kennedy; SCR: Melissa Mathison; PHOT: Allen Daviau; MUS: John Williams; CREATOR OF E.T.: Carlo Rimbaldi.

OSCARS: Best original score; best visual effects (Rambaldi, Dennis Muren, Kenneth F. Smith); best sound recording (Robert Knudson, Robert Glass, Don Digirolamo, Gene Cantamessa); best sound effects editing (Charles L. Campbell, Ben Burtt). OSCAR NOMINATIONS: Best film; best director; best screenplay; best cinematography; best film editing (Carol Littleton). (Winner best film 1982: *Gandhi*.)

115 minutes. Colour

Until *Titanic*, the most lucrative film ever made. At the last count it had taken more than 700 million dollars worldwide.

Frankenstein (1931)

The first Frankenstein movie was made by Thomas Edison in either 1908 or 1910 with one Charles Ogle playing the creature. One or two more silent versions followed but it was James Whale's 1931 production that proved definitive and, in effect, established the horror film genre. Bela Lugosi, who, earlier that year, had starred in *Dracula*, was offered the role of the

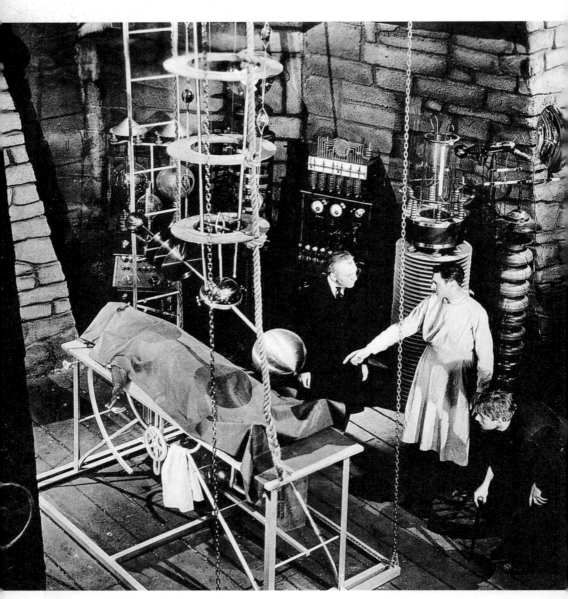

nameless monster but declined, thus leaving the way clear for a little-known English character actor, William Henry Pratt (a.k.a. Boris Karloff), to attain international renown at the age of 44. The original director, Robert Florey (replaced by another Englishman, James Whale), introduced the vital twist into the plot – instead of being provided with a normal brain the creature is given that of a madman. This, of course, left the way clear for the climactic slaughter and mayhem. Inevitably (in 1931 talking pictures were only four years old) the film has a certain primitive quality today, though the monster's make-up created by Jack Pierce – elongated brow, flat head, facial scars, bolts in the neck – has never been improved upon. But what makes this *Frankenstein* superior to all its numerous successors is the story-telling: we watch Karloff grow and change from the innocent, even sympathetic, creature to whom life has miraculously been given to the monster, rejected, misjudged and seething with all too potent frustration and rage. Because there is a build-up to the horror it is all the more shocking. Some of the sequences indeed were thought to be too shocking and it was not until 1987 when various key scenes were restored – among them the drowning of the little girl, a moment that could easily have been bathetic were it not so chillingly unexpected – that the full, uncensored version was shown.

MAIN CAST: Boris Karloff, Colin Clive, Mae Clarke, John Boles, Edward Van Sloan, Frederick Kerr, Dwight Frye. DIR: James Whale; PROD: Carl Laemmle, jun.; SCR: Garrett Fort, Francis Edward Farogoh, John L. Balderston (from the novel by Mary Wollstonecraft Shelley and the play by Peggy Webling); PHOT: Arthur Edson; MUS: David Broekman.

OSCAR NOMINATIONS: None. (Winner best film 1931–2: *Grand Hotel*.)

71 minutes. B&W

The creation (left) and the created, setting the pattern for countless remakes.

The General (1926)

Buster Keaton was the greatest of the silent comedians, greater than Chaplin because he eschewed the latter's irritating pathos. And *The General* was the greatest of his films – the greatest, some would argue (and it's not easy to contradict them) of all silent comedies. It's based loosely – very loosely – on a true incident during the American Civil War when a group of Union soldiers hijacked a railway engine (the eponymous General) from behind the Southern lines. (The Disney studios used the same basic story, to much less effect, in their 1956 *The Great Locomotive Chase*.) In Keaton's version he is the train's devoted engineer and doubly dismayed at the theft because his fiancée (Marion Mack) is aboard at the time. Heroically, therefore, he commandeers another engine to pursue the foul hijackers and rescue both his beloveds. The result is a matchless piece of wild, high-paced comedy, full of splendid sight gags and hair-raising stunts. Through it all Keaton maintains his familiar, slightly lugubrious deadpan; he might and indeed does feel emotion, but he never shows it – at least not facially; it's his remarkably

agile and graceful body that he allows to speak for him. *The General* is Keaton's masterpiece. He was never even to approach such heights again. In 1928 he left his own studio for MGM where he failed to adapt to the talkies and was soon rejected. He had been virtually forgotten until a retrospective in Paris in 1962 not only revived his films but led to a greater appreciation of them than they had enjoyed when they were first released.

Keaton, master of deadpan, sight gags and stunts, at his best in his own favourite film.

MAIN CAST: Buster Keaton, Marion Mack, Glen Cavender, Jim Farley, Frederick Vroom. DIR: Keaton, Clyde Bruckman; PROD: Joseph M. Schenck; SCR: Al Boasberg, Charles Smith; PHOT: J. Devereux Jennings, Bert Hains.

80 minutes. B&W. Silent

Genevieve (1953)

I was about to suggest that this was the kind of film only the British could make – until I remembered that the writer, William Rose, to whose script the picture's success owed so much, was an American. Nevertheless, in spirit, performance and execution *Genevieve* is essentially British or even, to narrow it down further, English. The charming middle-class manners (e.g. the scene when John Gregson nearly ruins his chances in the race by courte-ously allowing an enthusiastic old gent to bend his ear) are English; so are the breezy cheerfulness, the laconic understatement and the appealing lightness with which the whole question of sex is touched upon and, having been touched upon, is put very properly to one side. Naturally these two couples (Gregson and Dinah Sheridan, Kenneth More and Kay Kendall) are sexually interested in each other but, come, come, let's not dwell on it. The story is

The challenge (left) and the nail-biting climax as Genevieve lurches towards the finishing line.

sheer simplicity: two vintage car buffs, driving a 1904 Darracq (the eponymous Genevieve) and a 1904 Spyker and accompanied by their respective girlfriends, take part in the annual London to Brighton rally and then challenge each other to a race back to the capital, the prize being Genevieve herself. What transforms this from merely a likeable romp to an enduringly loveable comedy is the mysterious chemistry that sometimes occurs on movie sets and makes everything blend perfectly. The script is droll and witty; the pace, building up from a leisurely start, just right; and the performances, especially that of the trumpet-playing Kendall, are all that one could ask. Kendall, a delicious light comedienne, seemed to have the potential for international stardom and might well have achieved it had not leukaemia caused her tragically early death at the age of 33 in 1959. (Note: the music – a harmonica score composed and played by Larry Adler – was nominated for an Oscar. But because Adler was *persona non grata* with the House Un-American Activities Committee, the nomination was credited to – though never claimed by – Muir Mathieson. Academy records have since been changed to give Adler his due recognition.)

MAIN CAST: Kenneth More, John Gregson, Kay Kendall, Dinah Sheridan, Geoffrey Keen, Joyce Grenfell, Reginald Beckwith, Arthur Wontner. DIR/PROD: Henry Cornelius; SCR: William Rose; PHOT: Christopher Challis; MUS: Larry Adler; MUS DIR: Muir Mathieson.

OSCAR NOMINATIONS (1954): Best screenplay; best music. (Winner best film 1954: *On the Waterfront*.)

86 minutes. Colour

The Godfather (1972)

Godfather and family about to make someone an offer he can't refuse.

Quite simply the finest gangster film ever made, although morally disturbing in its presentation of the Mafia as, if not exactly the good guys, then at least worthy of our admiration. What, specifically, we are asked to admire are their sense of family and their loyalty to each other. Bearing in mind that the Mafia take care of their families and each other by means of organised crime and murder, this is a most specious argument, but in *The Godfather* it is put across with such brazen confidence that one finds oneself nodding agreement. What we are shown here is the dark side of the American Dream, a glamorous, ruthless group of people whose aspirations are precisely the same as those of legitimate big business, only their methods are a little different. Paramount (in the person of Robert Evans) chose the hitherto not particularly successful Francis Coppola to direct the film because he was of Italian origin and more likely to understand the society he was trying to depict. It was an excellent choice because Coppola delivered an extraordinary movie, a portrait of American free enterprise gone mad. Every scene, from the opening set piece to the massacre on the cathedral steps, teams with life (or death); the characters are vividly drawn and, yes, we do admire

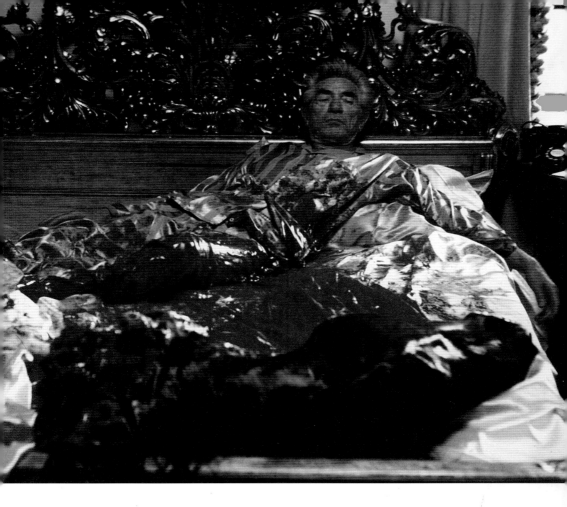

them and mourn with Brando and Pacino at the murder of Sonny (James Caan). Now, very well, deep down this is mere pulp fiction, but it's raised to epic proportions by a director who, at his best, is a genuine artist of the cinema. The grainy realism of the photography and Nino Rota's distinctive music – whose Oscar nomination was withdrawn when it was learned that part of the score had been used in the 1958 Italian film *Fortunella* – merely add further dimensions to what is already a masterly work.

MAIN CAST: Marlon Brando, Al Pacino, Robert Duvall, James Caan, Diane Keaton, Richard Castellano, Talia Shire, Richard Conte. DIR: Francis Coppola; PROD: Albert S. Ruddy; SCR: Coppola, Mario Puzo (from Puzo's novel); PHOT: Gordon Willis; MUS: Nino Rota.

OSCARS: Best film; best actor (Brando); best screenplay. OSCAR NOMINATIONS: Best director; best supporting actor (Pacino, Duvall, Caan); best costume (Anna Hill Johnstone); best sound recording (Bud Grenzbach, Richard Portman, Christopher Newman); best film editing (William Reynolds, Peter Zinner).

175 minutes. Colour

The Godfather Part II (1974)

For once the sequel is even better than the original. *Part II* is a fuller, deeper, more thoughtful film than *The Godfather,* being less an examination of organised crime and gang warfare than a chilling study of the way power corrupts. Even the cinematography is sharper, colder. Michael (Pacino) is now in command of the Corleone family and heading it towards respectability. No Brando here; instead we have Robert De Niro as the young Vito Corleone, whose early life is shown in flashback as he makes his way from Sicily through New York's Italian ghetto to the acquisition of power, the power which Michael inherits and uses ruthlessly to make the Corleone family paramount in Mafia circles. By the end of the film he has succeeded, but only at the cost of rejecting his wife (Keaton) and murdering both his brother-in-law and his own brother, Freddie (John Cazale). The argument that Michael does what he does (including fratricide) only for the good of the family is less convincing this time; nor, I think, are we meant to be convinced by it. His motive is ambition, the desire at any cost to control others. On his final, brooding appearance he is virtually omnipotent, having slaughtered all his rivals and enemies, but he is also alone, isolated by his own appalling achievements. In 1977 Coppola edited the two films together, adding nearly an hour of hitherto unseen footage, to make *The Godfather Saga* for television. To this, no doubt, will eventually be added *The Godfather Part III*, which he directed in 1990. This, too, is an entertaining movie but not in the same class as its predecessors; it has the same big, lavish look, but somehow misses the epic scale that made the others so outstanding.

MAIN CAST: Al Pacino, Robert De Niro, Diane Keaton, Robert Duvall, John Cazale, Lee Strasberg, Talia Shire, Michael V. Gazzo, Troy Donahue. DIR/PROD: Francis Coppola; SCR: Coppola, Mario Puzo; PHOT: Gordon Willis; MUS: Nino Rota.

OSCARS: Best film; best director; best screenplay; best supporting actor (De Niro); best art direction/set decoration (Dean Tavoularis, Angelo Graham, George R. Nelson); best music; best original music (Rota, Carmine Coppola). (*The Godfather Part II* was the first sequel ever to win the Oscar for best film.) OSCAR NOMINATIONS: Best actor (Pacino); best supporting actor (Strasberg, Gazzo); best supporting actress (Shire); best costumes (Theadora Van Runkle).

200 minutes. Colour

From father (De Niro, opposite) to son – power through corruption, corruption through power.

The Gold Rush (1925)

MAIN CAST: Charles Chaplin, Georgia Hale, Mack Swain, Tom Murray, Henry Bergman. DIR/PROD/SCR: Chaplin; PHOT: Rollie Totheroh, Jack Wilson. (Chaplin also composed the musical sound track, which he added, along with a narration, in 1942.)

72 minutes. B&W. Silent

Chaplin always presents me with difficulties. I admire his genius without necessarily finding it funny. His two- or three-reelers, fine; those I laugh at but not, as a rule, his feature films. Unarguably brilliant though he was, he struck me as a sprinter of a comedian rather than a middle-distance runner. But to all rules there are exceptions and in Chaplin's case *The Gold Rush* is chief among them. In 1958 an international jury in Brussels voted this the second greatest film ever made, only *Potemkin* being better. Now that is arguable, although Chaplin himself said that *The Gold Rush* was the film he would most like to be remembered for and it's not hard to see why. This tale of the gentle little fellow struggling to hold his own among his fellow prospectors – vast, unscrupulous brutes all of them – during the Klondike gold rush contains more comic invention than you could find in a dozen other movies. The house teetering on a precipice, for instance; the dance of the bread rolls; the boot which, in the torment of hunger, his imagination turns into a turkey dinner, the nails becoming bones to be sucked, the laces succulent strands of pasta. These are among the classic moments of the cinema and if they were not all entirely original, so what? As Olivier once said: 'Good actors borrow; great actors steal.' Chaplin was great enough, artist enough, to steal and then to turn the purloined material memorably into his own. Some of his later films, especially *A Countess from Hong Kong*, are best forgotten; *The Gold Rush* is unforgettable.

Chaplin and the edible boot – one of the
classic scenes of the cinema.

Gone with the Wind (1939)

It's quite possible that even today more people have seen *Gone with the Wind* than any other film. It was the film that brought the 1930s, the first and most successful decade of the Hollywood studio system, to a rousing climax; for sheer size and visual splendour nothing like it (except perhaps *The Birth of a Nation*) had ever been seen before. But its appeal to audiences lay elsewhere – in the way it took an enormous subject, the American Civil War, and made it the background to the adventures and misadventures of, essentially, four people. Thus it became an intimate spectacular, a small story told on an epic scale. It's therefore a movie set in the Civil War but not actually *about* the Civil War. That's going on all the time, of course, and most graphically is it illustrated (e.g. the aftermath of the battle of Atlanta), but apart from

knowing who's winning and who's losing we're not bothered with too many details. What concerns the film, and by extension us, is what's happening to Scarlett and Rhett (Vivien Leigh and Clark Gable) and Ashley and Melanie (Leslie Howard and Olivia de Havilland). Stories about the making of the picture have filled books: the role of Scarlett O'Hara was so coveted that almost every young female star inHollywood tested for it; David Selznick, however, eager to find a new face (and, of course, to gain maximum publicity) organised a nationwide two-year search for the perfect Scarlett before eventually signing the comparatively unknown Vivien Leigh; the original director, George Cukor, was replaced at Gable's insistence by Victor Fleming, who, because of illness, was in turn replaced by Sam Wood; writers as diverse as Scott Fitzgerald and Ben Hecht had a go at reducing Margaret Mitchell's book to filmable length; an early choice for Rhett Butler was Errol Flynn and so on. At the end of it all what emerged was a sumptuous, flamboyant entertainment, a cinematic novel – not a work of art perhaps but a rich, enjoyable wallow of a movie.

An idle thought: what difference would it have made if Errol Flynn (an early contender) had agreed to play Rhett Butler?

MAIN CAST: Clark Gable, Vivien Leigh, Olivia de Havilland, Leslie Howard, Thomas Mitchell, Hattie McDaniel, Butterfly McQueen, Evelyn Keyes, Ann Rutherford, Ward Bond. DIR: Victor Fleming (plus George Cukor, Sam Wood); PROD: David O. Selznick; SCR: Sidney Howard (from the novel by Margaret Mitchell); PHOT: Ernest Haller, Ray Rennahan; MUS: Max Steiner.

OSCARS: Best film; best actress (Leigh); best director (Fleming); best screenplay; best supporting actress (McDaniel); best cinematography; best art direction (Lyle Wheeler); best film editing (Hal C. Kern, James E. Newcom); plus Irving Thalberg Memorial Award to Selznick. OSCAR NOMINATIONS: Best actor (Gable); best supporting actress (de Havilland); best original score; best sound recording (Thomas T. Moulton); best special effects (John R. Cosgrove, Fred Albin, Arthur Johns).

220 minutes. Colour

La Grande Illusion (1937)

On the most obvious level Jean Renoir's masterly work is a cool yet passionate denunciation of war, a pacifist statement as strong as any made by *All Quiet on the Western Front*. The setting is a German POW camp in the First World War where the French prisoners dutifully occupy themselves with trying to escape. This, when you come down to it, is what war is about: men caged in by other men, men deprived of all right to freedom. But then you read the subtext and you discover that the film is also about something else again: it's about the passing of the old order, the aristocratic order that hitherto had ruled Europe; and it's about the class system itself. The upper-class French officer (Pierre Fresnay) has more in common with his fellow, albeit German, aristocrat (Erich von Stroheim), the commandant of the camp, than he does with his compatriots, the mechanic promoted from the ranks (Jean Gabin) and the Jew (Marcel Dalio). When he allows these two to escape by forcing the horrified von Stroheim to shoot him, he is acknowledging that patriotism takes precedence over class and that previously well-defined boundaries of class itself have become blurred. But there is a subtext even to the subtext because, once outside the camp, the escaping heroes revert to being blue-collar worker and despised Jew. The great illusion of the title – and of the conditions in the prison camp – is that the prejudices of class can easily be broken down. Superbly contrasting performances (the naturalness of Gabin, for instance, against the polished urbanity of

Fresnay and von Stroheim) give added pleasure to a film whose message is so subtly conveyed that, on the one hand, it was given a special prize in 1939 by the then notoriously Fascist Venice Film Festival and, on the other, it was banned by the Nazis.

Captivity brings the illusion of brotherhood; freedom (below) the reality that class distinction still exists.

MAIN CAST: Pierre Fresnay, Erich von Stroheim, Jean Gabin, Marcel Dalio, Julien Carette, Gaston Modot. DIR: Jean Renoir; PROD: Frank Rollmer, Albert Pinkovitch; SCR: Renoir, Charles Spaak; PHOT: Christian Matras, Claude Renoir; MUS: Joseph Kosma.

OSCAR NOMINATIONS (1938): Best film. (Winner best film 1938: *You Can't Take It with You*.)

117 minutes. B&W. French – subtitled with German and English characters speaking in their own languages

The Grapes of Wrath (1940)

The vivid realism and emotion with which John Ford brought Steinbeck's novel to the screen was such that towards the end even American audiences found themselves close to cheering the politics of the Left. That they didn't quite get there is due to the fact that the film betrays the climax of the book by introducing an upbeat ending extolling the basic goodness of working people as a whole, a concept which Americans found much more comfortable to applaud. Nevertheless, for most of the time *The Grapes of Wrath* justi-

fies the label 'great' that generations of critics have stuck on it. The story of the Joads, a family of sharecroppers driven from their Oklahoma farm when it becomes a dustbowl during the Depression years and trekking to California only to find that here is no promised land but merely greater poverty and even worse living conditions, is both a savage indictment of capitalist greed and a paean to the common man. In another mood, on another day Ford might easily have romanticised it; he did not. He might have sentimentalised it, but again, and save at the end, he did not. Instead, helped by powerful performances and Gregg Toland's magnificent camera-work, which starkly emphasises the abject conditions in which the migrants work and live, he presented an image of suffering, of poverty, of man's casual inhumanity to man, that at times has the disturbing immediacy of a documentary. There is anger in this film, a deep resentment of the social injustice and downright misery which America allowed to be visited upon thousands of its people. It was a remarkably brave and liberal picture to make at a time when the Dies Committee (forerunner of the House Un-American Activities Committee) was already trying to sniff out Communists in Hollywood.

MAIN CAST: Henry Fonda, Jane Darwell, John Carradine, Charley Grapewin, Dorris Bowdon, Russell Simpson. DIR: John Ford; PROD: Darryl F. Zanuck and Nunnally Johnson; SCR: Johnson (from the novel by John Steinbeck); PHOT: Gregg Toland; MUS: Alfred Newman.

OSCARS: Best director; best supporting actress (Darwell). OSCAR NOMINATIONS: Best film; best actor (Fonda); best screenplay; best sound recording (E.H. Hansen); best film editing (Robert E. Simpson). (Winner best film 1940: *Rebecca*.)

128 minutes. B&W

Fonda gaining his first Oscar nomination. He finally won the award with his last film, *On Golden Pond*, **in 1981.**

Great Expectations (1946)

The most astonishing aspect of David Lean's achievement is that he took Dickens's near-500-page novel, reduced it to less than two hours' screen time and yet lost so little that a great book became a great film. (If that doesn't impress you, compare the way Hollywood can take a slender book like *The Great Gatsby*, convert it into a 146-minute movie – and miss the essence of it.) Given a decent script – and the one provided was far more than that – the kind of consummate actors here assembled can be relied upon to fill in the richness and comic variety of Dickens's characters. The challenge to the director is in handling the storyline of such an intricately plotted novel and in this area Lean is totally in control. Inevitably (for the only alternative would have been a film about ten hours long) he cut the text; but having done so he did not simply

film what was left: he converted it into cinema – and that's something very different. Think of the sudden appearance of Magwitch in the graveyard, of Mrs Gargery's fierce upbraiding of Joe, of the fire that destroyed Miss Havisham. In Lean's hands these are not just moving illustrations of what Dickens described; they are the visual equivalents of Dickens's words and the effects were as graphic, startling, funny and exciting as the written passages. In other words, *Great Expectations* is not an adaptation – it's a superb translation of a magnificent tale with magnificent characters from one medium to another. (Note: As Herbert Pocket, Alec Guinness was making his film debut, apart from one day as an extra on the 1934 *Evensong*; and as Jaggers, Francis L. Sullivan reprised the role he played in the 1934 Hollywood version of *Great Expectations*.)

Pip's progress before, during and after the realisation of his great expectations.

MAIN CAST: John Mills, Bernard Miles, Finlay Currie, Martita Hunt, Jean Simmons, Valerie Hobson, Alec Guinness, Francis L. Sullivan, Anthony Wager. DIR: David Lean; PROD: Anthony Havelock-Allan; SCR: Lean, Ronald Neame, Havelock-Allan (from the novel by Charles Dickens); PHOT: Guy Green; MUS: Walter Goehr.

OSCARS (1947): Best cinematography; best art direction/set decoration (John Bryan, Wilfred Shingleton). OSCAR NOMINATIONS Best film; best director; best screenplay. (Winner best film 1947: *Gentleman's Agreement*.)

Gregory's Girl (1980)

Sinclair, Hepburn (not forgetting Forsyth) providing glorious proof that you don't have to spend a fortune to make a great film.

Of all the films listed here none can have had more humble origins than this one. It was made on a minuscule budget (about £200,000), much of it provided by the National Film Finance Corporation and Scottish Television, which latter connection would normally have categorised it as a TV movie launched by a brief theatrical run to satisfy the ego of its makers. Instead it turned out to be a little gem of a picture, now to be found on TV, certainly, but one whose natural home is the cinema. The shy, gawky Gregory (John Gordon Sinclair) loses his place in the school soccer team to a girl (Dee

Hepburn), but instead of resenting her he falls madly in love with her. And love is what we are talking about – not sex. Gregory and his friends are not the randy, smart-ass, self-important teenagers of so many Hollywood films; they're just a bunch of charming kids, growing up fast and slightly awed by their own emotions. In his portrait of Gregory's home life, his school, his extracurricular activities, Bill Forsyth does not introduce us to one remotely unpleasant person, either child or adult. There are no bullies, no drug problems, no sadistic teachers – just a bunch of totally believable, utterly

likeable people. What Forsyth seems to have (as he showed again later in the delightful *Local Hero*) is a life-enhancing belief in the innate decency of human nature. In *Gregory's Girl* that belief shines through to provide us with a film that, wittily, affectionately, touchingly and more effectively than any other I can remember evokes the bitter-sweet growing pains of adolescence.

MAIN CAST: John Gordon Sinclair, Dee Hepburn, Jake D'Arcy, Claire Grogan, Robert Buchanan, William Greenlees, Allison Forster, Chick Murray. DIR: Bill Forsyth; PROD: Davina Belling, Clive Parsons; SCR: Forsyth; PHOT: Michael Coulter; MUS: Colin Tully.

OSCASR NOMINATIONS: None. (Winner best film 1980: *Ordinary People*.)

91 minutes. Colour

Hannah and Her Sisters (1986)

Woody Allen is the most talented film maker now working in America and *Hannah and Her Sisters* is the best film he has made so far. There is a part of Allen that really wishes he were Ingmar Bergman; in its worst manifestation it produces *Interiors* (1978); in its best *Hannah*, a film that is plotted and constructed like a novel and in which a host of richly developed characters revolve around Hannah (Mia Farrow) and her sisters (Barbara Hershey and Dianne Wiest). Bergman could have made this picture, but he would have made it as a tragedy; so, probably, would the Allen of *Interiors*. Happily, this later – and, I like to think, more mature – Allen chose to make it not exactly as a comedy but as a very

funny drama. The potential for tragedy is there perhaps in the character of Hannah's ex-husband (Allen himself), who flutters around on the fringes, observing the activities of the others while morbidly agonising over his own mortality. But this is never allowed to darken the mood, just as the plentiful supply of typically sharp one-liners never disguises the fact that what we are watching is an essentially serious story of intricate relationships. The trappings of the tale are art and money, sex and ambition – success, Manhattan-style. The characters enjoy all these things and we enjoy them enjoying them. But what the film suggests – delicately, almost apologetically – is that while these people are pursu-

Two men in grave (and successful) pursuit of Oscars: Caine, the actor; Allen, the writer, possibly receiving news of his with typical exuberance.

ing what modern society deems to be the necessary accoutrements of a full life, they may be missing something more important. Allen has made funnier films; he has also made more earnest films. But he has never made one that probes so deeply and at the same time so delightfully as *Hannah*.

MAIN CAST: Woody Allen, Mia Farrow, Michael Caine, Carrie Fisher, Barbara Hershey, Dianne Wiest, Maureen O'Sullivan, Max Von Sydow, Lloyd Nolan, Sam Waterston, Tony Roberts, Daniel Stern. DIR: Woody Allen; PROD: Robert Greenhut; SCR: Allen; PHOT: Carlo di Palma; MUS: popular and classical standards.

OSCARS: Best screenplay; best supporting actor (Caine); best supporting actress (Wiest). OSCAR NOMINATIONS: Best film; best director; best set decoration (Carol Joffe); best film editing (Susan E. Morse). (Winner best film 1986: *Platoon*.)

107 minutes. Colour

High Noon (1952)

Carl Foreman, who wrote the script and is therefore worth listening to, claimed that *High Noon* was a political film: that Marshal Gary Cooper, abandoned by the townsfolk and (almost) by his bride (Grace Kelly) and waiting alone to confront the killers coming in on the noon train, actually represented the man of principle, deserted by his erstwhile friends and standing up to the House Un-American Activities Committee. The director, Fred Zinnemann, said Cooper represented nothing of the sort; he merely represented a man prepared to do what a man had to do. Well, it doesn't really matter, I suppose, although Foreman himself was blacklisted by HUAC. Nor does it matter that the story begins at 10.40 a.m. and ends at five minutes past noon, thus coinciding precisely with the film's running time. That's merely a gimmick, interesting but nothing to do with the quality of the picture. What finally makes *High Noon* a classic western is that it's so very well

done, stark in its simplicity. Not only was Cooper perfectly cast as the troubled lawman torn between the call of duty and the natural desire to go away with his lovely young wife, but the trappings of production, direction and script were also sublime – the menacing shadows cast by the blazing sun, the tension emphasised by the ticking of the clock, the almost palpable loneliness of the marshal as he realises that the honest burgers are going to rat on him. Even the bathetic lyrics of Tex Ritter's theme song ('He made a vow while in state prison/Said it'd be my life or his'n') were disguised by the darkly foreboding rhythm of the music. The western is the twentieth-century equivalent of the morality tale, the struggle between good and evil, what is right and what is wrong, and the dilemma has rarely been so plainly, so agonisingly laid out as in *High Noon*.

The marshal and his bride – 'Do not forsake me, oh my darling . . .'

MAIN CAST: Gary Cooper, Grace Kelly, Thomas Mitchell, Lloyd Bridges, Katy Jurado, Otto Kruger, Lon Chaney, Henry Morgan. DIR: Fred Zinnemann; PROD: Stanley Kramer; SCR: Carl Foreman (from *The Tin Star* by John W. Cunningham); PHOT: Floyd Crosby; MUS: Dmitri Tiomkin.

OSCARS: Best actor (Cooper); best music; best film editing (Elmo Williams, Harry Gerstad); best song ('Do Not Foresake Me', mus by Tiomkin, lyr by Ned Washington). OSCAR NOMINATIONS: Best film; best director; best screenplay. (Winner best film 1952: *The Greatest Show on Earth*.)

85 minutes. B&W

His Girl Friday (1940)

What is most noticeable about this (partially) transsexual adaptation of *The Front Page* is its pace. It fairly crackles along in a welter of verbal slapstick and overlapping dialogue, and it says much for both cast and director that it never becomes so fast as to be incomprehensible. *The Front Page* itself has been filmed twice – by Lewis Milestone in 1931 and by Billy Wilder in 1974. But neither of the, as it were, straight versions was as good or as successful as *His Girl Friday*, probably because what they lacked was the vital ingredient of sex, introduced here by the simple expedient of turning one of the two main protagonists, the ace reporter Hildebrand Johnson, into Hildegard Johnson (Rosalind Russell). At once the macho rivalry and bickering between Johnson and editor Walter Burns (Cary Grant) is converted into something much spicier – the battle of the sexes. Now Burns has a double reason for not wanting Hildy to leave town: not only would the paper have to find someone else to cover the hot murder story that's just breaking, but he would be losing (to Ralph Bellamy, her wimpish fiancé) his ex-wife – the woman he loves, the one he has found he can't live with but equally can't live without. Grant, stiff-legged, stiff-necked, roaring and ranting, and Russell, all long, elegant limbs and neat timing, are in terrific form, well supported by the chorus of journalists in the courthouse newsroom. Under Howard Hawks's impeccable direction this may not be (as some critics have claimed for it) the funniest comedy ever made but it's well up on the list – and if anyone makes a counterclaim that it's the fastest, I'm not going to argue. (In 1988 the same story, starring Kathleen Turner and Burt Reynolds, was transferred to a TV newsroom in *Switching Channels*. It didn't work.)

MAIN CAST: Cary Grant, Rosalind Russell, Ralph Bellamy, Gene Lockhart, Porter Hall, Ernest Truex, Clarence Kolb, Roscoe Karns, Frank Jenks. DIR/PROD: Howard Hawks; SCR: Charles Lederer (from *The Front Page* by Charles MacArthur and Ben Hecht); PHOT: Joseph Walker; MUS: Sydney Cutner.

OSCAR NOMINATIONS: None. (Winner best film 1940: *Rebecca*.)

92 minutes. B&W

Bellamy (wimpish), Grant (ranting), Russell (all legs and elegance) – *The Front Page* **with a spicy dash of sex.**

I Know Where I'm Going (1945)

A determined young woman (Wendy
Hiller) sets off for the western isles of
Scotland to marry her boss. He's old
enough to be her father and she doesn't
love him but he's rich and rich is what
she wants to be, too. She knows where
she's going. But virtually on the last leg
of her journey impenetrable fog
descends and she is unable to reach the
island where her fiancé is waiting for
her. After the fog comes a storm and
that, too, prevents her leaving the
mainland. In the meantime she has met
a young naval officer (Roger Livesey)
who is home on leave. He's obviously
attracted to her, but she resists him
because he doesn't appear to be rich
and she's not prepared to be side-
tracked by good-looking young men.
Thus begins a lyrical, even magical,
story which mingles romance, suspense
and comedy with a gentle touch of the
supernatural. As much as anything it
examines the effect of time and place
on people. The weather disrupts
Hiller's plans, but it's the mysterious
ambience of the countryside in which
she is virtually marooned that makes
her change them and realise that life
has more valuable things to offer than
money. A small, lovely film, beautifully
played and superbly photographed in
monochrome, it has a quality, a kind of
aftertaste, that lingers on in a way that
is almost disturbing and yet wholly
pleasurable. Rather touchingly, Michael
Powell chose the music from the film to
be played at his funeral.

**Wendy Hiller (second on right) learning
that money isn't everything – although,
conveniently she gets that, too.**

MAIN CAST: Wendy Hiller, Roger Livesey, Pamela Brown, Nancy Price, Finlay Currie, John Laurie. DIR/PROD/SCR: Michael Powell, Emeric Pressburger; PHOT: Erwin Hiller; MUS: Allan Gray.

OSCAR NOMINATIONS: None. (Winner best film 1945: *The Lost Weekend*.)

92 minutes. B&W

It Happened One Night (1934)

Once again what makes this mildly screwball romp one of the most endearing and enduring of romantic comedies is chemistry – in this case the chemistry produced by two stars who didn't want to make the film in the first place. Clark Gable indeed was in it only because he had offended Louis B. Mayer at MGM and was lent to Columbia as a punishment. And one can see why neither he nor Claudette Colbert was too keen on the picture. It's no more than a slender tale about a runaway heiress (Colbert) and an out-of-work journalist (Gable) who meet on a bus and fall in love. Yet it has delighted audiences for nearly sixty years, probably because these are the kind of attractive, humorous people we would like to be – or anyway would like to know. The setting is mainly rural America in the Depression era, but the tone is optimistic and cheerful, the incidental characters are pretty decent if sometimes more than a little bizarre and a deliciously sexy undercurrent runs through the whole film. Two scenes in particular remain in everyone's mind – the Walls of Jericho, when heiress and hack are forced to share a bedroom and coyly undress with a blanket suspended between them, and the hitchhiking contest when Colbert matches her legs against Gable's thumb. No contest at all, really. As handled by Colbert and the director, Frank Capra, that moment when she raises her skirt a few inches above the knee is more erotic than any amount of humping and grunting on beds.

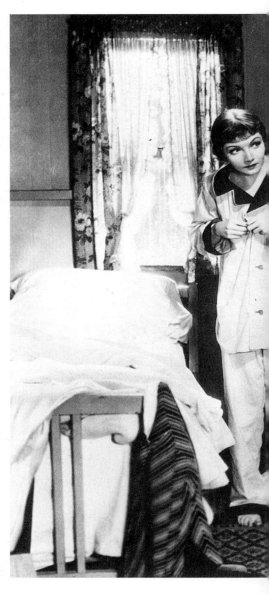

Colbert and Gable separated by 'the Walls of Jericho' – that impregnable blanket.

MAIN CAST: Clark Gable, Claudette Colbert, Walter Connolly, Roscoe Karns, Alan Hale, Ward Bond. DIR/PROD: Frank Capra; SCR: Robert Riskin (from *Night Bus* by Samuel Hopkins Adams); PHOT: Joseph Walker; MUS: Louis Silvers.

OSCARS: Best film; best actor (Gable); best actress (Colbert); best director; best screenplay. (The only other film to collect all those five most-coveted Oscar was *The Silence of the Lambs* in 1992.)

105 minutes. B&W

It's A Wonderful Life (1946)

Capra again but in a very different mood here. This is a film that people either love or hate. Depending on your point of view it's an unashamed statement to the innate goodness of humanity or alternatively it's sentimental goo. Cynics take the latter view and I'm sorry for them. James Stewart is the small-town philanthropist whose loan company has gone bust and who is saved from suicide by an elderly angel (Henry Travers), desperately trying to earn his wings. Stewart wishes he had never been born; Travers shows him what a hellhole his home town would have become without him. Capra is splendidly in control of his material throughout. Of course, such a story of supernatural intervention in the affairs of man could easily have tumbled into sentimentality – or worse – but it never does. An occasional, unexpected hard edge – Stewart railing furiously, illogically against his own family, for instance – makes a timely appearance to cut the sweetness. Capra's belief in the values of small-town America shines through but he never turns an

entirely unblinkered gaze upon them. Greed is the villain of the piece and there's at least a tacit acknowledgement that greed is one of the less desirable by-products of the American Dream, so the warm emotion of the film is tempered by some of the social consciousness that the director brought to *Mr Deeds Goes to Town* and *Mr Smith Goes to Washington*. *It's a Wonderful Life* is certainly simplistic and, if you like, naïve, but the doggedly optimistic message of the title is put across by both director and cast with such conviction as to be irresistible.

Stewart and Reed in a moment when life doesn't seem quite so wonderful.

MAIN CAST: James Stewart, Henry Travers, Donna Reed, Lionel Barrymore, Thomas Mitchell, Beulah Bondi, Gloria Grahame, Ward Bond, H.B. Warner. DIR/PROD: Frank Capra; SCR: Capra, Frances Goodrich, Albert Hackett; PHOT: Joseph Walker, Joseph Biroc; MUS: Dmitri Tiomkin.

OSCAR NOMINATIONS: Best film; best actor (Stewart); best director; best sound recording (John Aalberg); best film editing (William Hornbeck). (Winner best film 1946: *The Best Years of Our Lives*.)

129 minutes. B&W

Les Jeux Interdits (1952)
Forbidden Games

As an excoriating study of the effect of war and death on young children, this film stands in a class of its own. That it's an antiwar picture is evident from the early scenes – almost documentary in their sharpness – when German planes strafe a road crowded with refugees fleeing from Paris. From the carnage emerges a small girl, Paulette (Brigitte Fossey), her parents dead by the roadside. A peasant family takes her in and with their young son, Michel (Georges Poujouly), she begins to play the forbidden, even blasphemous, games of the title. The children create a cemetery for dead animals and because they know that graves need crosses they steal them from churches. So beautifully is this handled that it's some time before the heresy of what they are doing is brought home to us. But by then – or soon after – apparently bereaved relatives at a real funeral squabble and fight by the graveside and, compared with this, the basic innocence of the children's activities becomes startlingly clear. This is a deceptively simple film; it's about war and bereavement, but it's also about class (the difference between the bourgeois girl and the peasant boy) and it's about love – Michel's need for it and his ignorant parents' inability to show it. The parents are crudely depicted but we are grateful for that; without them the children's plight and our knowledge that they, too, must grow up to become part of the often cruel, often indifferent adult world would be almost unbearable.

The boy and the girl, divided by class, united by war and embarking upon their forbidden games.

MAIN CAST: Brigitte Fossey, Georges Poujouly, Amédée, Laurence Badie, Suzanne Courtal, Lucien Hubert, Jacques Marin. DIR: René Clément; PROD: Paul Joly; SCR: Clément, Jean Aurenche, Pierre Bost (from the novel by François Boyer); PHOT: Robert Julliard; MUS: Narciso Yepes.

OSCAR NOMINATION: Best original story (Boyer). SPECIAL AWARD: Outstanding foreign language film. (Winner best film 1952: *The Greatest Show on Earth*.)

84 minutes. B&W. French – subtitled

Kind Hearts and Coronets (1949)

Peter Ustinov once described *Kind Hearts* as perhaps Ealing Studios' 'most perfect achievement, a film of exquisite construction and literary quality'. It's usually lumped in with that glorious list of Ealing Comedies – one thinks of *Whisky Galore, The Man in the White Suit, A Run for Your Money, Passport to Pimlico* – and yet it's not at all like them. This is the atypical Ealing comedy, cool where the others were warm, sharply sophisticated where they were (in the best sense) simple. The joy of *Kind Hearts* lies as much in the spiky wit of the script as in the superb acting and the elegant, unobtrusive direction. For a start it's a great deal blacker than the other products of the Ealing stable, this story of a lowly haberdasher (Dennis Price) who murders his way towards the dukedom that, he feels, would rightfully have been his had not his mother made such an unfortunate marriage. Alec Guinness gives a formidable performance, or rather several formidable performances, as all eight of Price's victims, male and female, members of the luckless D'Ascoyne family who stand between the haberdasher and the peerage. As Ustinov said, it's a film that makes you want to read the script. ('I shot an arrow in the air; she fell to earth in Berkeley Square,' Price murmurs as he despatches one of his female kinsfolk, an intrepid balloonist.) This is a marvellously callous picture with no hint of sentimentality or remorse and brilliant both in its caricature of the aristocracy and its evocation of the Edwardian period. It's high comedy – steeped in English literary tradition and yet in no way merely a filmed book – written, directed and acted with an impeccable sense of style and cheerfully refusing (except at the very end where censorship insisted that Price must be punished) to pay any kind of lip service to moral convention.

MAIN CAST: Dennis Price, Alec Guinness, Valerie Hobson, Joan Greenwood, Miles Malleson, Arthur Lowe. DIR: Robert Hamer; PROD: Michael Relph; SCR: Hamer, John Dighton (from the novel *Noblesse Oblige* by Roy Horniman); PHOT: Douglas Slocombe; MUS: Mozart's *Don Giovanni*.

OSCAR NOMINATIONS: None. (Winner best film 1949: *All the King's Men*.)

106 minutes. B&W

Guinness (with Price and Hobson) in two of the eight roles which, in only his third film, confirmed his formidable reputation.

The Lady Eve (1941)

This is probably the high point of the brief but glorious directorial career of Preston Sturges – a deliciously sexy comedy set on a luxury liner with Barbara Stanwyck as a professional

cardsharp and Henry Fonda her selected victim, a millionaire scientist who is more comfortable with snakes than with women. Mind you, the way she behaves there doesn't seem to be a lot of difference. Sturges's gift was the rare ability to combine high verbal comedy with wild visual slapstick and the mixture never worked better than it does here. Stanwyck, so often the sultry *femme fatale*, was allowed to reveal her full, and too often neglected, comic range as, too, was Fonda. The plot, of course, is nonsense and doesn't bear deep analysis, but the same is true of *Bringing Up Baby* and *It Happened One Night*, with both of which *The Lady Eve* compares very favourably.

The moral, if there is one, is that given a sparkling cast and a highly talented director even nonsense can be raised to a delightful level. Sturges, variously described as 'the streamlined Lubitsch' and 'the Breughel of American comedy directors', was a late-flowering wonder boy, a writer-director who was at his peak with the eight films he made between 1940 (when he was 42) and 1944. Among these were *The Great McGinty*, *Sullivan's Travels* and *The Miracle of Morgan's Creek*. But after that he left Paramount and went to work for Howard Hughes and somewhere along the line the magic vanished. How dazzling that magic could be can be seen by comparing *The Lady Eve* with the dull 1956 remake *The Birds and the Bees*, featuring George Gobel, David Niven and Mitzi Gaynor. None of these was any kind of substitute for Stanwyck and Fonda, but what the remake lacked most sorely was Preston Sturges.

MAIN CAST: Barbara Stanwyck, Henry Fonda, Charles Coburn, Eugene Pallette, William Demarest, Eric Blore. DIR/SCR: Preston Sturges (adapted from the play by Monckton Hoffe); PROD: Paul Jones; PHOT: Victor Milner; MUS: Leo Shuken, Charles Bradshaw.

OSCAR NOMINATION: Best original story (Hoffe). (Winner best film 1941: *How Green Was My Valley*.)

97 minutes. B&W

The cardsharp with entourage (right) and prospective mark (left) before the dictates of romantic comedy showed her the error of her ways.

The Lady Vanishes (1938)

On a transcontinental train an elderly lady (Dame May Whitty) suddenly disappears. The only passenger who has seen her – or admits to having seen her – is Margaret Lockwood, who, being young and beautiful, manages to persuade the smitten but initially reluctant Michael Redgrave to join her in a search for the missing party. Villains conspire to thwart them as, more innocently, do Basil Radford and Naunton Wayne, the very embodiment of a pair of silly ass Englishmen anxious to return home in time for the Manchester Test Match. With this mélange of spies and secret, coded messages, of tension, melodrama, danger and sheer, exuberant fun, Hitchcock (aided by an excellent script) was at his incomparable best. *The Lady Vanishes* (which, incidentally, offered Redgrave his first starring role) is not perhaps Hitch's most famous film; *Psycho* almost certainly claims that distinction. But it demonstrates all the director's noted ingenuity, imagination and ability to shock

along with an engaging quality of warmth that was far less apparent in much of his later work. And (as in the case of *The Adventures of Robin Hood*) it is imbued with conviction and enthusiasm. The 1979 remake, starring Cybill Shepherd and Elliott Gould, failed largely because it was played tongue-in-cheek. If even the actors couldn't take it seriously, why should the audience?

MAIN CAST: Margaret Lockwood, Michael Redgrave, May Whitty, Basil Radford, Naunton Wayne, Paul Lukas, Cecil Parker, Catherine Lacey, Linden Travers, Googie Withers. DIR: Alfred Hitchcock; PROD: Edward Black; SCR: Frank Launder, Sidney Gilliat (from the novel *The Wheel Spins* by Ethel Lina White); PHOT: Jack Cox; MUS: Louis Levy.

OSCAR NOMINATIONS: None. (Winner best film 1938: *You Can't Take It with You*.)

97 minutes. B&W

The shoot-out on the train – just another
ploy to keep Radford and Wayne from ever
getting to the Test Match?

Laura (1944)

As the critic Pauline Kael has said, *Laura* is 'everybody's favourite chic murder mystery'. But it's more than just that, more even than a classic *film noir*. It's both an ingenious thriller and, in its own way, an affectionate examination of the thriller's conventions. The action gets under way when a detective (Dana Andrews) falls in love with the picture of a beautiful girl

(Gene Tierney), whose apparent murder he is investigating. Ah, but has she really been murdered – and, if not, where is she? The film opens with a soliloquy by Clifton Webb, as a superbly mannered and cynical newspaper columnist, and proceeds to unfold partly in flashback. The question hovering over what transpires is not simply whodunit but whodunwhat and why. Is there a touch of necrophilia in Andrews' obsession with Laura; or a hint of voyeurism in the investigation of the girl's life? Well, yes – or anyway, maybe. The script is lean and literate, the direction (by Otto Preminger, who took over from Rouben Mamoulain) coolly skilful and the characters are both mysterious and complex, there being – in the tradition of *film noir* – more to all of them than meets the eye. The immediate success of the film did much to establish the careers of both Webb and Preminger.

MAIN CAST: Dana Andrews, Clifton Webb, Gene Tierney, Vincent Price, Judith Anderson, Dorothy Adams, James Flavin. DIR/PROD: Otto Preminger; SCR: Jay Dratler, Samuel Hoffenstein, Betty Reinhardt (from the novel by Vera Caspary); PHOT: Joseph La Shelle; MUS: David Raksin.

OSCAR: Best cinematography. OSCAR NOMINATIONS: Best director; best screenplay; best supporting actor (Webb); best art direction/interior decoration (Lyle Wheeler, Leland Fuller, Thomas Little). (Winner best film 1944: *Going My Way*.)

88 minutes. B&W

Detective Andrews (centre) perhaps realising that he is in a *film noir* and there's more to this than meets the eye.

The Lavender Hill Mob (1951)

The great charm of the Ealing Comedies (of which this, I suggest, is the most enduringly popular) is that they were insular without being parochial. The story of a meek, middle-aged bank messenger (Alec Guinness), who plans and pulls off a £3,000,000 bullion robbery, is so constructed as to be essentially English. Of course, it could be transposed to New York, Paris or any other city you care to name, but it would lose a lot in the translation. Somehow it *needs* London and the particular characters assembled in 'the mob': Guinness's

archetypal bank clerk, Stanley Holloway's genteel second in command, Sidney James's and Alfie Bass's half-smart Cockney wide boys – their direct equivalents are not to be found anywhere else. And yet, having admitted the insularity, one must also acknowledge the universality of the tale. It's the little man's, Everyman's, dream of how to get rich quick, the perfect crime in which nobody is hurt and, in a way, nobody is the loser except, alas, the mob themselves. The cinema morality of the time, which insisted sternly that crime must not be seen to pay, gave the film its bitter-sweet ending. It's a neat enough pay-off but it's not the ending the audience wants, for by the time it arrives we know these people so well and like them so much that we are desperate for them to get away with it. If the movie was made today, they would and we would like them no less for their triumph than we did for their failure. After all, consider another crime caper, *A Fish Called Wanda*, which the same director (Charles Crichton) made thirty-seven years later. In this John Cleese and Jamie Lee Curtis fly off happily with their ill-gotten loot – and our complete approval – to much the same part of South America from which Guinness was returned in handcuffs. Incidentally, in *The Lavender Hill Mob's* early South American scenes you may recognise a little-known starlet named Audrey Hepburn. I wonder whatever became of her?

MAIN CAST: Alec Guinness, Stanley Holloway, Sidney James, Alfie Bass, Marjorie Fielding, John Gregson, Edie Martin, Gibb McLaughlin. DIR: Charles Crichton; PROD: Michael Truman; SCR: T.E.B. Clarke; PHOT: Douglas Slocombe; MUS: Georges Auric.

OSCAR (1952): Best screenplay. OSCAR NOMINATION: Best actor (Guinness). (Winner best film 1952: *The Greatest Show on Earth*.)

82 minutes. B&W

Guinness and Holloway concocting their master plan to turn the stolen gold into miniature Eiffel Towers.

Lawrence of Arabia (1962)

with all its mystery and menace, the real star of the picture. Never is this more apparent than in the famous sequence in which Sharif, starting as a small speck in the far distance, gallops endlessly, grippingly, towards the camera. That scene, which is even longer in Lean's restored and re-edited 1989 version than it was in the original, emphasises the director's vision, his remarkable eye for the spectacular and his courage. On the obvious level the story, adapted loosely from *The Seven Pillars of Wisdom*, concerns T. E. Lawrence's accomplishments in leading the Arab revolt against the Turks, Germany's allies, in the First World War. But equally it's a study of the enigmatic Lawrence himself, a man both socially and sexually unconventional, a hero unlike any other. It's this that makes *Lawrence* by far the best and least patronising of all modern epics because in the end what Lean and Bolt give us is an intimate, personal story told on a vast scale – an enormous canvas dominated by one man. Lean's choice of the unknown O'Toole to play that man was, like his shot of Sharif approaching across the desert, a case of courage rewarded. For O'Toole, who won the role only after Albert Finney declined it, gave a most impressive performance.

The remarkable thing about *Lawrence,* is that it contains hardly any of the ingredients that normally go to make up an epic. It has comparatively few leading characters, little in the way of subplot to clutter up the narrative, no love interest, no big names in the leading roles (Peter O'Toole and Omar Sharif were hardly known then) and not really a great deal of action. What it has instead is a spare but intelligent script by Robert Bolt and David Lean's boldness in making the desert itself,

MAIN CAST: Peter O'Toole, Omar Sharif, Arthur Kennedy, Jack Hawkins, Alec Guinness, Donald Wolfit, Claude Rains, Anthony Quayle, Anthony Quinn, Jose Ferrer, Michel Ray, Zia Mohyeddin. DIR: David Lean; PROD: Sam Spiegel; SCR: Robert Bolt; PHOT: Freddie Young; MUS: Maurice Jarre.

The desert as star. After every shot an army of workers swept the sand to prepare for the next take.

OSCARS: Best film; best director; best cinematography; best art direction/set decoration (John Box, John Stoll, Dario Simoni); best music; best sound recording (John Cox); best film editing (Anne Coates).
OSCAR NOMINATIONS: Best actor (O'Toole); best supporting actor (Sharif); best screenplay.

222 minutes (1962); 216 minutes (1989). Colour

The Leopard
Il Gattopardo (1963)

When the young Burt Lancaster first met Shelley Winters he said (or so it is alleged): 'You don't think much of me, do you?' to which Winters replied: 'Not at all, Mr Lancaster. I think you're a very fine acrobat.' Well, in those days that's what he was. But by the time he played Prince Fabrizio in *The Leopard* he had also become a very fine actor. He gives the performance of his life as an ageing, dying aristocrat looking back with nostalgic regret at the decline of his class. The focal point of the film is Garibaldi's expedition to unite Sicily with Italy by deposing King Francis II. It's a time of political upheaval – the end of the aristocracy, the rise of the masses – and Lancaster is no less affected than anyone else. In particular he is hurt by the fact that his son (Alain Delon) is to marry a parvenue (Claudia Cardinale), daughter of the local mayor. He sees change and decay all around and he doesn't like any of it. There is a curious ambivalence in the picture because Visconti, himself an aristocrat but also a professed Marxist, appears almost to share the prince's view. This is a democratic revolution as seen by someone opposed to it and Visconti, who would have agreed with it, is nevertheless honest enough to show that even a democratic revolution can seem a pretty shabby thing. The spectacular climax, the marriage ball at which for the first time (certainly in the prince's house) the classes mingle freely, is a marvellously ironic comment on the breakdown of the old social order. There, as indeed throughout, meticulous attention to detail superbly evokes a portrait of a rich and once powerful society in terminal decline. When 20th Century Fox first released *The Leopard* in Britain and the US, it was clumsily dubbed, cut by forty-four minutes and the prints, made by a Fox subsidiary, so enraged Visconti that he disclaimed authorship of this international version. Fortunately, however, in 1983 some reparation was made when the film was reissued with many of the cuts restored. But there is still no subtitled version available.

MAIN CAST: Burt Lancaster, Claudia Cardinale, Alain Delon, Paolo Stoppa, Serge Reggiani. DIR/SCR: Luchino Visconti (adapted from the novel by Prince Giuseppe de Lampedusa); PROD: Goffredo Lombardo; PHOT: Giuseppe Rotunno; MUS: Nino Rota.

OSCAR NOMINATION: Best costume design (Piero Tosi). (Winner best film 1963: *Tom Jones*; winner best foreign language film 1963: Federico Fellini's *8½*.)

205 minutes (in Italian). 161 minutes (dubbed version). 186 minutes (1983 reissue). Colour

Lancaster, the aristocrat, marking the transition from former circus performer to later four-time Oscar nominee.

The Maltese Falcon (1941)

Remarkably, this is a remake – or, if you like, even a second remake. Dashiell Hammett's thriller was first filmed with Ricardo Cortez and Bebe Daniels in 1931 and again, in a much reworked version, as *Satan Met a Lady* with Warren William and Bette Davis in 1936. But John Huston's film – his first as a director – totally eclipsed both the others. With its brilliant, if fortuitous, casting of Humphrey Bogart, who was chosen only after George Raft had refused to work with a debutant director, it took the detective thriller into a new dimension. Bogart's Sam Spade was the prototypical antihero, a cynical romantic as tough, mercenary and ruthless as any of the crooks who oppose him. This was his best role since *The Petrified Forest* in 1936 and the one that firmly established his now familiar screen persona. Furthermore the film introduced the 62-year-old British stage actor Sydney Greenstreet to the screen as the jovially sinister fat man, a role he continued to play throughout the decade. And beyond all that it could be argued that with its congregation of shady, equivocal characters, its sharp, sardonic humour, its atmosphere redolent of darkness, betrayal and perversion and its moody, brooding use of black and white photography, *The Maltese Falcon* was the forerunner of all those *films noirs* that came along a few years later. It is in many ways a significant movie, but if it were that alone it would by now be merely a footnote in books of cinematic history. That it has avoided such a fate is due to the fact that it's also marvellous entertainment, beauti-

fully played and most skilfully crafted. (The story was reworked yet again in 1975 as *The Black Bird*, a weak parody starring George Segal and Stéphane Audran.)

MAIN CAST: Humphrey Bogart, Mary Astor, Sydney Greenstreet, Peter Lorre, Elisha Cook, jun., Barton MacLane, Gladys George, Ward Bond. DIR/SCR: John Huston (adapted from the novel by Dashiell Hammett); PROD: Henry Blanke; PHOT: Arthur Edison; MUS: Adolph Deutsch.

OSCAR NOMINATIONS: Best film; best screenplay; best supporting actor (Greenstreet). (Winner best film 1941: *How Green Was My Valley*.)

100 minutes. B&W

Almost inconceivable now that the original choice to play Sam Spade was George Raft.

M.A.S.H. (1970)

The initials, of course, stand for Mobile Army Surgical Hospital and Robert Altman's film became what Mike Nichols's adaptation of *Catch 22* (also in 1970) should have been but failed to be – the landmark antiwar comedy of its time. Certainly the two surgeons, Donald Sutherland and Elliott Gould, though up to their elbows in the blood and guts of wounded American soldiers during the Korean War, appear to be having a very good time with their moonshine and cruel jokes at the expense of Hotlips Houlihan and her illicit lover. But there is always a desperate note to the frivolity, which itself serves as a counterpoint to the noisy, frenetic horror that is going on all around them. Altman once told me that the ideal film is one which simply cannot be described in words

alone and *M.A.S.H.* comes close to fulfilling that definition. It's a visceral, emotional assault that has to be felt as well as seen and heard, a wildly funny, uneven, unsentimental, enormously energetic attack on almost everything that the American Establishment, or any nation's Establishment, holds dear. On the surface it's total lunacy; underneath what it peddles is grim sanity. The humour is fast and spiky with one-liners matching, topping and often overlapping each other and there's a nervous, edgy quality to script, performances and direction that keeps you constantly aware that though the film might be funny, war is not, a point that was often lost in the otherwise agreeable and long-running TV spin-off starring Alan Alda.

What was expected was a jolly wartime romp; what Robert Altman delivered was a comedy with fangs.

MAIN CAST: Donald Sutherland, Elliot Gould, Sally Kellerman, Tom Skerritt, Robert Duvall, Jo Ann Pflug, Rene Auberjonois. DIR: Robert Altman; PROD: Ingo Preminger, Leon Ericksen; SCR: Ring Lardner, jun. (from the novel by Richard Hooker); PHOT: Harold E. Stine; MUS: Johnny Mandel.

OSCAR: Best screenplay. OSCAR NOMINATIONS: Best film; best director; best supporting actress (Kellerman); best film editing (Danford B. Greene). (Winner best film 1970: *Patton*.)

116 minutes. Colour

A Matter of Life and Death (1946)

The theme, of a man summoned to death before his time and fighting, as it were, for a stay of execution, had been well worked over in the 1941 *Here Comes Mr Jordan*. But Powell and Pressburger were never much inhibited by what had been done before; they merely did it again and did it better. *A Matter of Life and Death* is one of those rare films that stays indelibly in the mind, in part because of its passion and exuberance, its plea (as timely now as it was in 1946) for greater understanding between nations and its belief in the power and joy of love. Corny stuff maybe but, when reaped by masters, corn can be golden all the way through. David Niven is the RAF pilot who miraculously escapes alive when he jumps, without the benefit of a parachute, from his burning plane; Kim Hunter the American radio operator with whom he falls in love. Later the action moves from the Technicolor of earth to the monochrome of heaven – the two linked by a giant, metaphorical escalator – as Roger Livesey defends Niven's right to another chance at life and Raymond Massey, an embittered veteran of the American War of Independence, opposes it. Even today this is a dazzling film, a fantasy, a satire, a love story, a thoughtful examination of English mysticism and romanticism that combines the verbal wit and visual flair that we expect from Powell and Pressburger with a use of colour and special effects that is still impressive in an age when computerised technology is so advanced as to dominate modern cinema.

MAIN CAST: David Niven, Kim Hunter, Roger Livesey, Raymond Massey, Marius Goring, Abraham Sofaer. DIR/PROD/SCR: Michael Powell, Emeric Pressburger; PHOT: Jack Cardiff; MUS: Allen Gray; PROD DESIGN: Hein Heckroth.

OSCAR NOMINATIONS: None. (Winner best film 1946: *The Best Years of Our Lives*.)

104 minutes. Colour

Niven, Hunter (opposite) and the heavenly trial that will grant him life or death.

Mean Streets (1973)

Martin Scorsese is the most gifted and versatile director currently working in the American cinema, one who appears to be influenced far less by commercial considerations than by a desire to make the movies he believes in. This, though only his third film, is still, I think, his best so far – less disturbing than *Taxi Driver*, less polished than *Goodfellas* but exuding a rare sense of honesty and reality. The story of two young hoodlums (Robert De Niro and Harvey Keitel) trying to establish themselves in the lower levels of the New York Mafia is hardly autobiographical but seems to be based on what Scorsese learned and observed as he himself grew up in Little Italy, the stronghold of the Manhattan mob. This is a gangster story without doubt, but even more it's about growing up and adapting in a gangster-dominated environment where people drift into the Mafia because that's all there is, because it's the family business – everyone's family business. Of the two protagonists Keitel, a collector for his uncle's protection racket, is the realist; De Niro the wild romantic seemingly more influenced by Mafia myth and Mafia movies than by the actuality around him. He is the violent one whom Keitel, a devout Catholic despite everything, tries to protect. This is a doomed couple and, as in all good tragedies, we know that from the start. The story is strong and unusual, but what makes it special is the beautifully observed setting in

De Niro's first film with Scorsese. They have since made five more together.

which Scorsese has placed it and the utterly credible atmosphere of petty crime, boredom, sudden violence and small, snatched pleasures with which he surrounds his characters. There is nothing mannered or stylised; even the eruptions of violence look natural and almost clumsy and Keitel and De Niro are such convincing small-time losers that we come to feel that this is not so much a work of the imagination as events remembered.

MAIN CAST: Robert De Niro, Harvey Keitel, David Proval, Amy Robinson, Richard Romanus, Robert Carradine, David Carradine (and Scorsese himself as the gunman in the car). DIR: Martin Scorsese; PROD: Jonathan Taplin; SCR: Scorsese, Mardik Martin; PHOT: Kent Wakeford; MUS: Various sources.

OSCAR NOMINATIONS: None. (Winner best film 1973: *The Sting.*)

110 minutes. Colour

Modern Times (1936)

Technically, I suppose, this is Chaplin's first sound movie in that he does utter sounds, not words, just sounds – deliberate gibberish as he impersonates a singing waiter. (Perhaps we should be grateful for the gibberish. When in 1940 he finally delivered a comprehensible speech – his plea for world peace in *The Great Dictator* – it was notable mostly for its pompous naivety.) *Modern Times*, Chaplin's first film since *City Lights* five years earlier, is for the most part a disjointed, episodic, fairly obvious but still very funny satire on industrial technology and its dehumanising effects, a topic no less pertinent now than it was then. In Chaplin's demonic factory one machine sucks him into its works, another force-feeds him with soup and corn on the cob and if he so much as pauses for a quick scratch, total chaos ensues. The satire is broad rather than deep, good-natured rather than savage, but even so it annoyed American industrialists and caused the picture to be banned as Communist propaganda in Germany and Italy. The love interest is most engagingly provided by Paulette Goddard and, happily, Chaplin's pathos and sentimentality are held on a tighter rein than usual. The film was influenced by René Clair's *A Nous la Liberté*, whose production company, having come under Nazi control, was persuaded by Dr Goebbels to sue for plagiarism. But since Clair was only too pleased to acknowledge his own debt to Chaplin the case faded away. *Modern Times* is perhaps the most loosely constructed of Chaplin's features but it is, nevertheless, a classic of visual comedy.

Chaplin with Goddard. He married her, but then he often married his leading ladies – a sort of tradition he had.

MAIN CAST: Charles Chaplin, Paulette Goddard, Chester Conklin, Henry Bergman, Tiny Sandford. DIR/PROD/SCR: Chaplin; PHOT: Rollie Totheroh, Ira Morgan; MUS: Chaplin.

OSCAR NOMINATIONS: None. (Winner best film 1936: *The Great Ziegfeld*.)

89 minutes. B&W

My Darling Clementine (1946)

When John Ford was making his silent westerns Wyatt Earp would turn up on the set and, among other thinks, get drunk with the cowboy extras. Thus *My Darling Clementine* is based to some extent on Earp's own account (or, more accurately, the way Ford remembered it) of what happened at the gunfight at the OK Corral. A classic, low-key western, vividly imbued with the director's romantic, nostalgic conception of what life might have been like in a tough frontier town such as Tombstone. Of the many screen versions of the famous gunfight this is possibly the most accurate and certainly the most memorable though, oddly enough, what stays in the mind even more than the gunfight itself is the build-up to it. Henry Fonda's portrait of Earp as a quiet, almost shy man, a gunslinger turned law enforcer determined to make the West a place where decent folks could live, is admirably sustained and cleverly developed in a series of vignettes – Earp at the barber's shop or reclining on the porch, the dance in the church and many more. The chief supporting players, led by Walter Brennan as the head of the ill-fated Clanton family, are extremely (and, in the case of Victor Mature as the consumptive Doc Holliday, surprisingly) good. Ultimately, Ford may – as he preferred – have printed the legend but close attention to period detail and splendid camera work provide at least the look and feel of authenticity.

MAIN CAST: Henry Fonda, Victor Mature, Walter Brennan, Linda Darnell, Cathy Downs, Tims Holt, Ward Bond, Alan Mowbray, John Ireland. DIR: John Ford; PROD: Samuel G. Engel; SCR: Engel, Winston Miller (from *Wyatt Earp, Frontier Marshal* by Stuart Lake); PHOT: Joseph P. MacDonald; MUS: Cyril Mockridge.

OSCAR NOMINATIONS: None. (Winner best film 1946: *The Best Years of Our Lives*.)

98 minutes. B&W

Earp reclining on the porch when – before the gunfight – Tombstone was at least a quiet place for folks to live.

Napoleon (1927)

Of all existing versions of this truly
magnificent film, the best is surely the
five-hour version lovingly recreated in
1981 by Kevin Brownlow, with later
assistance from Bambi Ballard. So
much material has been lost or mislaid
that it's still not complete and, alas,
probably never will be but what there is
of it is astounding. Abel Gance's

admiring view of Napoleon as a super-man of destiny may not appeal to everyone (least of all historians) but the telling of his life story, from childhood to the entry into Italy, is masterly. Gance used just about every existing screen technique – from hand-held camera to wide-angle lens, from tinting and superimposition to a (then) new and stunning triple-screen effect for the final climactic scenes – to extend the boundaries of film-making. Anyone who still doubts that film can be art has not seen *Napoleon*. Gance origi-nally planned to make six films, in total nine hours long, covering the whole of Bonaparte's life but his entire budget – and far more – was spent on the one. That he did not complete the project is much to be regretted; on the other hand the picture he did make is to be treasured. Gance was finishing *Napoleon* even as Warner Brothers were making the first talkie, *The Jazz Singer*. The latter is now a curiosity; the former is a film of grace, power and visual imagery that has rarely – if ever – been equalled. The initial accompanying musical score was by Arthur Honegger. The score for the Brownlow version was composed by Carl Davis.

MAIN CAST: Albert Dieudonné, Antonin Artaud, Gina Manes, Pierre Batcheff, Wladimir Roudenko, Nicolas Koline. DIR/SCR: Abel Gance; PROD: WESTI/Société Générale de Film; PHOT: Jules Kruger.

OSCAR NOMINATIONS: None. (Winners best films 1927–8: *Wings and Sunrise*.)

300 minutes approx. B&W (with some colour). Silent

In 1927 Abel Gance was 38. He continued making films until 1963 but nothing else he did came close to matching *Napoleon*.

Nashville (1975)

Here, as in *M.A.S.H.*, we have Robert Altman freewheeling, playing with the medium and, this time, cramming the screen with a multitude of different characters and themes as he presents us with a little world of his own creation. This is an idiosyncratic, satirical vision of America, its politics, its music, its lifestyle, the whole summed up in a line from one of the songs: 'We must be doing something right to last 200 years.' It's a film that is, at the same time, a send-up, a country and western musical, a narrow look at Nashville itself and a study of the relationship between audience and performers. There is no single star – just a crowd of people of more or less equal importance. What distinguishes Altman – and also perhaps accounts for the fact that he is one of the most underrated of American directors – is the liberality with which he sprays out his ideas. His best films are never merely about one thing; they attempt to be all-embracing and this accounts both for their richness and their unevenness. The starting point for *Nashville* is a pop concert organised in support of a mammoth political rally and that's the excuse for the camera to follow the separate, in one case tragic, and overlapping activities of at least a couple of dozen people, among them Elliot Gould and Julie Christie appearing as themselves. It amounts to an almost epic portrait of America in the 1970s, in the course of which some gloriously spiky fun is had at the expense of the characters and, even more, of the nation itself.

Robert Altman's second notable tilt at the windmills of the US Establishment. With *The Player* **(1992) he added Hollywood to his victims.**

MAIN CAST David Arkin, Ned Beatty, Barbara Baxley, Ronee Blakley, Geraldine Chaplin, Keith Carradine, Shelley Duvall, Allen Garfield, Henry Gibson, Keenan Wynn, Lily Tomlin, Scott Glen, Jeff Goldblum. DIR/PROD: Robert Altman; SCR: Joan Tewkesbury; PHOT: Paul Lohmann; MUS: Richard Baskin.

OSCAR: Best song ('I'm Easy', mus/lyr by Keith Carradine). OSCAR NOMINATIONS: Best film; best director; best supporting actress (Blakley, Tomlin). (Winner best film 1975: *One Flew Over the Cuckoo's Nest*.)

159 minutes. Colour

The Nights of Cabiria
Le Notti di Cabiria (1957)

Fellini at his best with an apparently, and artfully, unstructured-looking film in which, finally, everything falls precisely into place. Giulietta Masina (as good as, if not better than, she was in *La Strada*) is the prostitute, no longer young, who is thrown into the water by her lover, rescued, taken up by a famous actor and generally exploited. At a music hall she is hypnotised by a magician and talks so innocently and touchingly about her youth and her dreams that a young man in the audience proposes to her. But little enough comes of that for the young suitor, too, takes advantage of her and in the end she is more or less back where she began. The contrast between the streetwalker's tough, knowing surface and her inner naïvety, even purity, between her adolescent aspirations and the rackety life she leads is beautifully explored. This is Fellini looking outward rather than inward, as he was increasingly to do with the likes of *8½* and *Roma* and it is less vividly spectacular than most of his later works. In scale *The Nights of Cabiria* is a comparatively small film but it is none the less impressive for that. The same story, very much adapted, was used in the stage musical *Sweet Charity* which, in turn, was filmed in 1969 with Shirley MacLaine as the prostitute.

MAIN CAST: Giulietta Masina, François Périer, Amadeo Nazzari, Franca Marzi. DIR: Federico Fellini; PROD: Dino De Laurentiis; SCR: Fellini, Ennio Flaiano (additional dialogue by Pier Paolo Pasolini); PHOT: Aldó Tonti; MUS: Nino Rota.

OSCAR: Best foreign language film. (Winner best film 1957: *The Bridge on the River Kwai*.)

110 minutes. B&W. Italian – subtitled

Fellini's poignant Cinderella story which proves that modern fairy tales don't necessarily have a happy ending.

Ninotchka (1939)

First, with *Anna Christie* (1930), we had the slogan: 'Garbo talks!' For *Ninotchka* the hypeline was 'Garbo laughs!' as if the unhappy woman had never done so before. Never mind. She does indeed laugh quite joyously (although rumour has it that the actual sound was provided by some anonymous stand-in) in the course of a radiant performance that combines sensuality with an unexpectedly delicate touch of comedy. Of all her movies – *Queen Christina* notwithstanding – this is my favourite simply because it's such fun and because Garbo brings to it such a deliciously understated eroticism. She plays a Soviet commissar sent to Paris to bring back three comrades who have been seduced by Western materialism, only to suffer much the same fate herself as she falls for the suave Melvyn Douglas. Script and direction alike sparkle with sharp one-liners and a hard-edged cynicism which, with its patronising suggestion that Russian idealism could easily be bought for a smart hotel suite, room service and a few bottles of champagne, might easily have become offensive. That it does not and that the film maintains a level of highly sophisticated light comedy is due largely to the performances – and most of all Garbo's. Melvyn Douglas provides an ideal foil in a role for which the earlier contenders were William Powell and Robert Montgomery. The story was later adapted for the stage and screen musical *Silk Stockings*, with Fred Astaire and Cyd Charisse in the 1957 film version.

Douglas to Garbo: 'Never did I dream I could feel like this toward a sergeant.'

MAIN CAST: Greta Garbo, Melvyn Douglas, Ina Claire, Bela Lugosi, Sig Rumann, Felix Bressart, Alexander Granach, Gregory Gaye. DIR: Ernst Lubitsch; PROD: Sidney Franklin; SCR: Charles Brackett, Billy Wilder, Walter Reisch (from a story by Melchior Lengyel); PHOT: William Daniels; MUS: Werner Heyman.

OSCAR NOMINATIONS: Best film; best actress (Garbo); best screenplay; best story. (Winner best film 1939: *Gone with the Wind*.)

110 minutes. B&W

Oh! Mr Porter (1937)

The superb Will Hay was one of the greatest – and today, alas, is one of the most neglected – of British screen comedians and this is his, well, masterpiece is perhaps too heavy a word to hang on such a flimsy structure. On the other hand merely to say that *Oh! Mr Porter* is his best and funniest picture is not really to say enough. This is a little jewel of a film, an exuberant romp in which everything knits seamlessly together and in which every scene has its share of delights. In fact there's not a duff moment in any of them. Hay, in his familiar character of the confident but utterly incompetent bungler trying to come to grips with a job he doesn't even understand, is the railwayman in charge of the derelict and reputedly haunted Bugleskelly railway station. With him, ostensibly to provide assistance but effectively just getting in the way, are his two regular henchmen, Moore Marriott and Graham Moffatt.

The story, which involves gun runners and a wildly funny climax on a runaway railway engine, was heavily influenced by, if not lifted from, *The Ghost Train,* but the script was meticulously tailored to fit the talents and exquisite timing honed by Hay and company during their years in music hall. The whole film is so well constructed, so delightfully played that even today it has a vitality and freshness that few modern comedies can equal.

MAIN CAST: Will Hay, Moore Marriott, Graham Moffatt, David O'Toole, Sebastian Smith, Dennis Wyndham, Agnes Lauchlan. DIR: Marcel Varnel; PROD: Edward Black; SCR: Val Guest, J.O.C. Orton, Marriott Edgar; PHOT: Arthur Crabtree; MUS: Louis Levy.

OSCAR NOMINATIONS: None. (Winner best film 1937: *The Life of Emile Zola.*)

84 minutes. B&W

Will Hay (with henchmen and feathered friend) – one of the screen's great comedians.

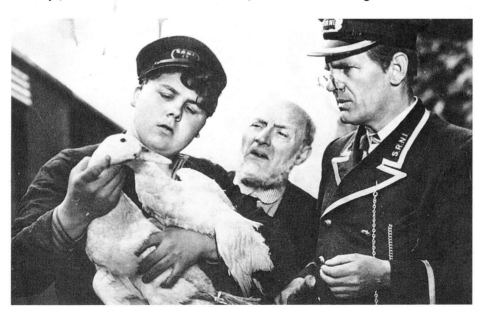

On The Waterfront (1954)

A classic piece of realist drama, filmed on location in New York, and one of the most powerful films of its decade, which incorporates possibly Marlon Brando's finest performance and certainly Rod Steiger's. Brando is the ex-boxer ('I coulda been a contender') who, through a variety of circumstances including the murder of his corrupt brother (Steiger), stands alone against Lee J. Cobb's Mafiosi, who control New York's waterfront. Both the writer, Budd Schulberg, and the director, Elia Kazan, had testified before the House Un-American Activities Committee and Brando's final transition from perceived stool pigeon to defiant hero is sometimes interpreted as their justification for their own actions. Whether this is so or not is unimportant, though it gives an added point of interest. Brando's performance as the inarticulate former pug whose inherent decency forces him, reluctantly, to take on the hoodlums is magnificent. And yet, in the much-parodied car scene wherein he delivers the 'contender' speech, he is almost acted off the screen by Steiger, appearing in only his second film. But then the entire cast is excellent and for once the Method style of acting, which they all embrace, is exactly right. Schulberg, who wrote the script from Malcolm Johnson's Pulitzer Prize-winning articles about the work of a Jesuit priest (played by Karl Malden), later developed his screenplay into a novel and gave it a more downbeat, but undoubtedly more likely, ending. An introductory note to the film claims optimistically that corruption can be beaten by constitutional means; Schulberg's novel suggests realistically that it can't.

MAIN CAST: Marlon Brando, Eva Marie Saint, Lee J. Cobb, Rod Steiger, Karl Malden, Pat Henning, Lief Erickson, James Westerfield, John Hamilton. DIR: Elia Kazan; PROD: Sam Spiegel; SCR: Budd Schulberg; PHOT: Boris Kaufman; MUS: Leonard Bernstein.

OSCARS: Best film; best actor (Brando); best director; best screenplay; best supporting actress (Saint); best cinematography; best art direction (Richard Day); best film editing (Gene Milford). OSCAR NOMINATIONS: Best supporting actor (Cobb, Steiger, Malden); best music.

108 minutes. B&W

Brando's Oscar was the first of two he has won. Four of his eight nominations came in the first seven films.

Pat and Mike (1952)

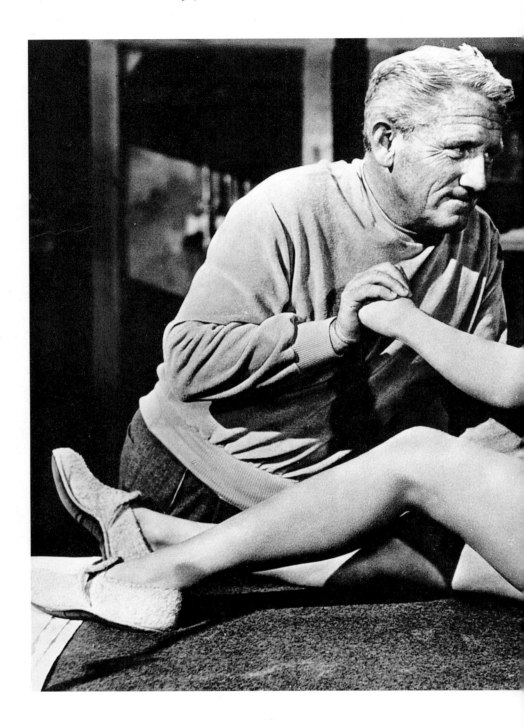

The attraction of opposites – on screen and in life. The love affair between Hepburn and Tracy ended only with his death.

The Hepburn-Tracy team at their peak. *Adam's Rib* may have been wittier but *Pat and Mike* is funnier, affording endless opportunities for two of the most talented screen actors Hollywood has ever produced to bring out the best in each other. There are echoes here of *Woman of the Year*, the first movie they made together, for as in that one, Hepburn is the cool, well-bred socialite and Tracy the streetwise plebeian, here frustrated by petty crooks from pursuing the honest career he would prefer. This time, however, Hepburn is a phenomenal all-round athlete, good enough at both tennis and golf to take on and beat the best in the world; Tracy is the small-time sports' promoter whose stable, until she comes along, consists mainly of a petulant and usually horizontal heavyweight (Aldo Ray). 'There's not much meat on her,' says Tracy, contemplating his new client, 'but what there is is cherce.' And cherce – or, if you prefer, choice – is the comedy and conflict that ensues from the pairing of this ill-assorted yet perfectly matched duo. Their graceful, effortless performances are splendidly orchestrated by George Cukor, who was just about peerless at handling this kind of material.

MAIN CAST: Spencer Tracy, Katharine Hepburn, Aldo Ray, William Ching, Jim Backus, Sammy White, Phyllis Povah. DIR: George Cukor; PROD: Lawrence Weingarten; SCR: Ruth Gordon, Garson Kanin; PHOT: William Daniels; MUS: David Raksin.

OSCAR NOMINATION: Best screenplay. (Winner best film 1952: *The Greatest Show on Earth*.)

95 minutes. B&W

Panther Panchali (1955)

This is cheating really because, good as it is, *Panther Panchali* (Little Song of the Road) is still best appreciated when seen as one-third of what has come to be known as the 'Apu' trilogy. The two later films are, in their own way, just as impressive, but I choose *Panther Panchali*, Satyajit Ray's first picture, because it was a quite astonishing debut. It tells of the birth and growing up of young Apu in an impoverished Bengali village and is, in essence, a remarkably ordinary tale, a tale of rural life and of family and community relationships. But Ray's brilliance was such that he could take this simple material and mould it so skilfully that he was able to give us a richly charming picture of the joy and wonder of childhood and, at the same time, make India more accessible, more understandable, to the Western world. There is, in particular, one lovely scene – perhaps the most vivid in the entire film – of Apu and his sister racing to catch a glimpse of a passing train. That in itself tells us more about the remoteness and the unsophisticated life of the villagers than many directors could get across in an entire movie. Ray's brand of lyrical, even magical, realism was a sharp break from the escapist tradition

Director Satyajit Ray's charming portrayal of life in an impoverished Bengali village established him as one of the cinema's outstanding original talents.

of Indian cinema. Apu and his family are the core of the film but the most memorable character is the octogenarian storyteller played by the veteran actress Chunibala, who took the part largely because the wages would feed her daily drug habit. *Panther Pachali* was based on the first of three novels by Bhibuti Bashan Bannerjee. Ray completed his, and the author's, trilogy with *Aparajito* (*The Unvanquished*) (1956) and *Apur Sansar* (*The World of Apu*) (1959). In these he follows Apu's progress as, after the death of his father, he makes his way to university, enters into an arranged marriage, suffers the death of his mother and his wife and, after many vicissitudes, comes through shaken but unbeaten. If *Panther Panchali* is outstanding in the trilogy it's because, being the first, it was the most startling and unexpected from an Indian director. But all three are imbued with Ray's warmly affectionate belief in mankind's ability to learn and grow.

MAIN CAST: Subir Bannerjee, Kanu Bannerjee, Karuna Bannerjee, Uma Das Gupta, Chunibala. DIR/SCR: Satyajit Ray (from the novels by B.B. Bannerjee); PHOT: Subrata Mitra; MUS: Ravi Shankar.

OSCAR NOMINATIONS: None. Foreign language films were not nominated until 1956. Satyajit Ray was awarded a special Oscar for services to the cinema shortly before he died in 1992. (Winner best film 1955: *Marty*.)

122 minutes. B&W. Bengali – subtitled

Paths Of Glory (1957)

The film that announced Stanley Kubrick's arrival as a director of remarkable ability. It has been described as 'one of the most powerful antiwar films ever committed to cellu- loid', but it is even more than that: it is, above all, a scathing, angry attack on the military mentality. Three soldiers are chosen as scapegoats to be court- martialled for cowardice after the

bloody failure of a cynically ill-conceived attack on an impregnable German position during the First World War. Captain Dax (Kirk Douglas), the officer detailed to defend these men, provides the moral heart of the film. As in *La Grande Illusion* the crux of the story lies in the virtually unbridgeable class distinction between the French officers and men, a division illustrated with bitter irony in the contrast between officers jockeying for promotion behind the lines and the slaughter of the cannon fodder in the trenches. The pitiless attitude of the higher military echelons, who are prepared to sacrifice anyone of lower rank to protect themselves, is superbly mirrored in the equally pitiless way in which Kubrick exposes the moral corruption of these people. The grimness

of the story would be almost intolerable were it not for the honesty and compassion of Dax, who provides a necessary quality of decency against which to measure the self-seeking cruelty of the generals. The underlying theme – the brutalising effect of war – is one to which Kubrick has twice returned, with *Dr Strangelove* and *Full Metal Jacket* but, admirable as both those films are, *Paths of Glory* covers the subject with greater and more chilling effect.

SCR: Kirk Douglas, Adolphe Menjou, George Macready, Ralph Meeker, Timothy Carey, Wayne Morris, Richard Anderson. DIR: Stanley Kubrick; PROD: James B. Harris; SCR: Kubrick, Calder Willingham, Jim Thompson (from the novel by Humphrey Cobb); PHOT: Georg Krause; MUS: Gerald Fried.

Kirk Douglas (left, with Adolphe Menjou) as the officer torn between loyalty to his class and the dictates of justice.

OSCAR NOMINATIONS: None. (Winner best film 1957: *The Bridge on the River Kwai*.)

86 minutes. B&W

Psycho (1960)

My initial reaction to seeing *Psycho* was that all it amounted to was three blood-chilling moments – the shower scene, the attack on the landing, the mummified corpse in the basement – held together by nothing very much. All subsequent viewings have (a) not only underlined the astonishing impact of those sequences, but (b) have persuaded me that I can't have been paying enough attention the first time around. *Psycho*, which Hitchcock once described as 'my first horror film', is in fact a superbly structured thriller. It's a pretty heartless one, for it was made when the director appeared to have abandoned warmth for a macabre fascination with the darker aspects of evil, but from its quiet opening (Janet Leigh embezzling her employer's funds and beating it out of town) to its shocking climax it is most artfully put together. Hitchcock cheats outrageously – of

course he does. The traffic cop's inscrutable sunglasses, for example, lead to sinister expectations that are not fulfilled, nor was there ever any intention that they should be. False trails abound; car number plates are given a significance that they never deserve. All this was simply the master toying with his audience, playing it along, deluding it, misdirecting it, confident in the knowledge that when the big moments came they would frighten the life out of everyone in the cinema. There are Hitchcock films for which I have a far greater affection than *Psycho* but there is no shock/horror movie which is more compulsively watchable. It is outrageously manipulative, its subject matter is essentially banal and yet it is not too much to describe it as the work of a genius. By comparison its sequels, with which Hitchcock had no connection, are beneath consideration.

MAIN CAST: Anthony Perkins, Vera Miles, John Gavin, Janet Leigh, Martin Balsam, John McIntire, Simon Oakland. DIR/PROD: Alfred Hitchcock; SCR: Joseph Stefano (from the novel by Robert Bloch); PHOT: John L. Russell; MUS: Bernard Herrman.

OSCAR NOMINATIONS: Best director; best supporting actress (Leigh); best cinematography; best art direction/set decoration (Joseph Hurley, Robert Clatworthy, George Milo). (Winner best film 1960: *The Apartment*.)

109 minutes. B&W

Anthony Perkins as Norman Bates, a name now synonymous with evil, and the spooky house he inhabited behind the Bates Motel.

Pulp Fiction (1994)

With his first two films – *Reservoir Dogs* followed by this – Tarantino reinvented the thriller for the modern age. *Pulp Fiction* is an astonishing entertainment, a whirligig of violence, blood, sudden death, sex, comedy and wit, that cheerfully and unashamedly has no more moral depth than its title would suggest. Within an intriguingly circular framework Tarantino weaves together three interconnecting stories which seem to come straight from the pages of pulp magazines. A young couple (Roth and Plummer) are planning to hold up a diner; a pair of hitmen (Travolta and Jackson) are on their way to kill some yuppies who have been foolish enough to try to double-cross their boss; a boxer (Willis) reneges on an agreement to take a dive. Around

every story as each goes its separate way, occasionally brushing up against one of the others, is woven a rich tapestry of incidental characters and detail – a petty crook is accidentally shot in the back of a car and Keitel is called in to clean up the mess; the boss's girlfriend (Thurman) overdoses, almost fatally, on heroine; the boss himself (Rhames) is snatched and raped by a couple of weirdoes; and so it goes. The story begins and ends in the same place – the diner – at the same time, but between the opening shot and the closing credits we have learned what is going to happen to some of the characters later in the day. Tarantino has a marvellous eye and ear and the courage, rarely found in modern thriller makers, to let his characters talk to each other – Travolta

John Travolta's career skyrocketed. Probably the biggest come-back in cinema history

and Jackson, for instance, postponing their hit while they finish an earnest discussion on the difference between rubbing a woman's foot and cunnilingus. This is a wickedly inventive film that creates a world of its own, a world in which none of the people seems real and yet each is totally believable. It also, incidentally, made Tarantino a cult figure and effected a Lazarus-like resurrection of the career of John Travolta.

MAIN CAST: John Travolta, Samuel L. Jackson, Bruce Willis, Uma Thurman, Tim Roth, Amanda Plummer, Harvey Keitel, Ving Rhames, Maria De Madeiros, Eric Stoltz, Rosanna Arquette, Christopher Walken. DIR: Quentin Tarantino. PROD: Lawrence Bender. SCR: Tarantino, Roger Avar;. PHOT: Andrzej Sekula.

OSCAR: Best screenplay. OSCAR NOMINATIONS: Best picture; best director; best actor (Travolta); best supporting actor (Jackson); best editing (Sally Menke). (Winner best film 1994: *Forrest Gump*.)

153 minutes. Colour

Pygmalion (1938)

Shaw's sophisticated comedy of class and manners – to say nothing of bad manners, Professor Higgins being capable of shocking rudeness – brought most elegantly to the screen. This production, without doubt the best film version of any of G.B.S.'s plays, has been much overshadowed by the later success of *My Fair Lady*. One can see why: *M.F.L.* had the music, the colour, Cecil Beaton's costumes, a great wad of Oscars and an enormous budget. Even so Pygmalion is much the more reward-ing film. By concentrating on the play, rather than adorning it, it emphasised the wit, irony and social satire in a way that *M.F.L.* missed. More than that, it gave the tall and gifted Wendy Hiller her first leading film role. Julie Andrews was fine on stage as Eliza in *M.F.L.*, Audrey Hepburn less so in the movie, but Hiller, admittedly granted more of the text to get her teeth into, gave the definitive performance. As Higgins, Leslie Howard – though not called upon to sing, or rather declaim,

which was probably to his advantage – is more than a match for Rex Harrison. *Pygmalion* is a film that owes its sublime confidence to a distinguished cast which, Howard apart, had very little experience of the movies but which had been reared on the stage classics. It was a great and immediate success in America and it says much for its abiding appeal that when *My Fair Lady* was made, *Pygmalion* was withdrawn from circulation. Presumably the expectation was that comparisons between the old and the new would be detrimental to the latter and if so, that was not a bad guess.

MAIN CAST: Leslie Howard, Wendy Hiller, Wilfred Lawson, Marie Lohr, Scott Sunderland, Jean Cadell. DIR: Anthony Asquith, Leslie Howard; PROD: Gabriel Pascal. SCR: George Bernard Shaw (from his play), adaptation by W.P. Lipscomb, Cecil Lewis, Ian Dalrymple; PHOT: Harry Stradling; MUS: Arthur Honegger.

OSCAR: Best screenplay and adaptation. OSCAR NOMINATIONS: Best film; best actor (Howard); best actress (Hiller). (Winner best film 1938: *You Can't Take It with You*.)

96 minutes. B&W

Never mind *My Fair Lady*, **this was the best screen version of** *Pygmalion* **– with Shaw's Oscar to prove it.**

Raging Bull (1980)

A number of America's leading critics voted this the best film of the 1980s, which is perhaps a little over the top, although I do see their point. It's based on the life of Jake La Motta (Robert De Niro), a slum kid who fought his way out of the Bronx to become middleweight boxing champion of the world, earned and wasted several small fortunes and, in a curious sort of

comeback, re-emerged as a sadly inept stand-up comedian. What is so striking about the film is the way it captures the raw energy and simmering anger of the subject himself. It makes little attempt to delve inside him and indeed the impression given is that there would have been little to find there anyway. La Motta, who was involved in the production of the picture, is portrayed as a man not much given to introversion, a primitive force who wears his emotions on the outside and is most distinguished by a gift for violence which, though useful in his chosen trade, destroys his private life. To a large extent his nemesis is his beautiful teenage wife (Cathy Moriarty), his obsession with whom drives him into paroxysms of self-induced jealousy. He has no understanding of women; to him they are either sluts or goddesses and sometimes both. This is a visceral film, fast, exciting, often brutal both in the fight scenes and in the way it associates sexuality with violence, and handled with immense confidence by Martin Scorsese. De Niro, who took dedication to his craft so far as to put on 60lb to play the older, fatter La Motta, is outstandingly good as a man in whom rage, frustration and bewilderment struggle for supremacy; not a likeable man perhaps, but one ultimately deserving of our sympathy or even pity.

MAIN CAST: Robert De Niro, Cathy Moriarty, Joe Pesci, Frank Vincent, Nicholas Colosanto, Theresa Saldana, Frank Adonis. DIR: Martin Scorsese; PROD: Robert Chartoff, Irwin Winkler; SCR: Paul Schrader, Mardik Martin; PHOT: Michael Chapman; MUS: library sources.

OSCARS: Best actor (De Niro); best film editing (Thelma Schoonmaker). OSCAR NOMINATIONS: Best film; best director; best supporting actor (Pesci); best supporting actress (Moriarty); best cinematography; best sound recording (Donald O. Mitchell, Bill Nicholson, David J. Kimball, Les Lazarowitz). (Winner best film 1980: *Ordinary People*.)

128 minutes. Colour and B&W

Martin Scorsese lost the best director Oscar to Robert Redford (*Ordinary People*). Future generations will continually wonder why.

Ran (1985)

The genesis of *Ran* was a sixteenth-century Japanese legend about a warlord who divided his lands among his three sons and retired to live in peace. To this Kurosawa added aspects of Shakespeare's *King Lear*, discarding the daughters but retaining the Fool, plus samurai costumes and make-up inspired by Noh drama. The result is not peace but (as the title roughly translates) chaos. It is also an astonishing epic, a work of sumptuous visual grandeur that encompasses the elements of human drama and tragedy – love, greed, hatred, grief. Kurosawa described his film as 'human deeds as viewed from heaven' and sure enough there is a sense of distance in his telling of the tale. Havoc ensues when the great warlord (Tatsuya Nakadai)

divides between his sons the kingdom he had earlier won by virtue of his own bloody conquests. From them he demands – and by the first two is glibly given – an oath of loyalty. Only the youngest (Daisuke Ryu), who loves his father most and who is disgusted by his brothers' hypocrisy, refuses. Ironically therefore it is he – the Cordelia figure – who arouses the parental wrath and by the time the warlord realises his error it is too late, for chaos (superbly illustrated in colourful, stylised battle scenes as the brothers make war upon each other) has destroyed the kingdom. All this we observe both from above and yet, at the same time, through the eyes of the horrified warlord as he scurries, stripped of his power, humiliated and driven to madness, through the appalling carnage his actions have unleashed. *Ran* is a stunningly vigorous and imaginative film, all the more remarkable for the fact that Kurosawa, who had spent ten years raising the finance, was 75 when he made it.

MAIN CAST: Tatsuya Nakadai, Satoshi Terao, Jinpachi Nezu, Daisuke Ryu, Mjeko Harada, Yoshiko Miyazaki, Masayuki Yui. DIR: Akira Kurosawa; PROD: Serge Silberman, Masato Hara; SCR: Kurosawa, Hideo Oguni, Masato Ide; PHOT: Takao Saito; MUS: Toru Takemitsu.

OSCAR: Best costume design (Emi Wada). OSCAR NOMINATIONS: Best director; best cinematography; best art direction (Yoshiro Muraki, Shinobu Nuraki). (Winner best film 1985: *Out of Africa*; winner best foreign language film: *The Official Story*.)

161 minutes. Colour. Japanese – subtitled

In the West *Ran* confirmed Kurosawa's status as a master; in Japan he is still merely regarded as a commercial movie maker.

Rashomon (1951)

This was the film which, when shown at the 1951 Venice festival, truly awakened Western interest in Japanese cinema in general and Akira Kurosawa in particular. A bandit, coming upon a couple in the forest, kills the husband (a samurai) and rapes the wife. All fairly straightforward – but is it? For we are told the same story from different points of view – the bandit's, the wife's, the dead husband's and that of a woodcutter who had secretly witnessed the whole thing. All the versions are different but which is the true one? What indeed is truth? And why do people lie – out of malice or because they tailor events to fit their own image of themselves? The death of the husband, for instance, could be murder, suicide or the result of a more or less fair fight. Little by little as the contrasting stories unfold we learn more about each of the characters but the problem is: what should we believe? As much as anything Kurosawa seems to be concerned with the nature of people who cannot exist without lies because the lies, the blurring of the facts, are essential to their self-esteem. *Rashomon* is a fascinating, sometimes savage, film, most artfully directed and photographed and played in a deliberately mannered style that emphasises the element of fantasy in each of the several stories. A little masterpiece, which was transposed into something far less than that in the 1964 Hollywood version, *The Outrage*, starring Paul Newman.

The film which established Kurosawa with Western audiences as the most accessible of Japanese directors.

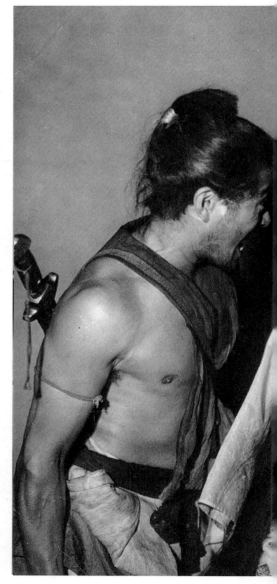

MAIN CAST: Toshiro Mifune, Machiko Kyo, Masayuki Mori, Takashi Shimura. DIR: Akira Kurosawa; PROD: Jingo Minoura; SCR: Kurosawa, Shinobu Hashimoto (from stories by Ryunosuke Akutagwa); PHOT: Kazuo Matsuyama; MUS: Takashi Matsuyama.

SPECIAL AWARD: Outstanding foreign language film. (Winner best film 1951: *An American in Paris*.)

88 minutes. B&W. Japanese – subtitled

Red River (1948)

John Ford's reaction upon first seeing John Wayne (whom he had directed many times) in *Red River* was: 'I never knew the sonofabitch could act.' It was not the least of Howard Hawks' achievements that he elicited from Wayne a far better performance than the one which, much later, won him his only Oscar in *True Grit*. *Red River* is about a mid-nineteenth-century cattle drive along the newly opened Chisholm Trail, an enterprise beset by stampedes, gunfights, Indian raids and the conflict between Wayne and his adopted son, Montgomery Clift. Just as these days westerns tend to appear in a different guise (*Star Wars*, for example, is basically a western), so adventure stories from other genres can easily be adapted to the west and in a broad sense *Red*

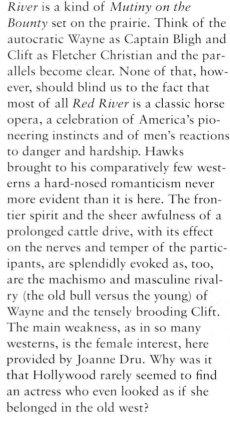

River is a kind of *Mutiny on the Bounty* set on the prairie. Think of the autocratic Wayne as Captain Bligh and Clift as Fletcher Christian and the parallels become clear. None of that, however, should blind us to the fact that most of all *Red River* is a classic horse opera, a celebration of America's pioneering instincts and of men's reactions to danger and hardship. Hawks brought to his comparatively few westerns a hard-nosed romanticism never more evident than it is here. The frontier spirit and the sheer awfulness of a prolonged cattle drive, with its effect on the nerves and temper of the participants, are splendidly evoked as, too, are the machismo and masculine rivalry (the old bull versus the young) of Wayne and the tensely brooding Clift. The main weakness, as in so many westerns, is the female interest, here provided by Joanne Dru. Why was it that Hollywood rarely seemed to find an actress who even looked as if she belonged in the old west?

MAIN CAST: John Wayne, Montgomery Clift, Joanne Dru, Walter Brennan, Colleen Gray, John Ireland, Noah Beery, jun., Harry Carey, jun. DIR/PROD: Howard Hawks; SCR: Borden Chase, Charles Schnee (from Chase's story 'The Chisholm Trail'); PHOT: Russell Harlan; MUS: Dmitri Tiomkin.

OSCAR NOMINATIONS: Best original story (Chase); best film editing (Christian Nyby). (Winner best film 1948: *Hamlet*.)

133 minutes. B&W

The young bull (Clift with the miscast Joanne Dru) and the old (Wayne in classic, heroic pose).

The Red Shoes (1948)

There are those who regard *The Red Shoes* as the finest achievement of the Powell-Pressburger partnership. There are many more for whom it is the most perfect ballet film ever made and yet others who see it as the ideal backstage musical. All these are matters for debate, but what is beyond question is that this is a breathtakingly imaginative film, an attempt to fuse music, dance and drama with a brilliant command of movie technique into something that comes as close as possible to total cinema. And yet the peg on which all the pyrotechnics are hung is a slender one, Hans Christian Andersen's cruel story – illustrated in a fourteen-minute ballet – of the girl whose red shoes will not let her stop dancing until she dies. The film's plot is simply another version of Andersen's tale. The subject had first been considered ten years earlier with Merle Oberon in mind but in the event the ballerina Moira Shearer, making her screen debut, played the young dancer so in love with her art and so torn by the conflicting demands of her domineering impresario (Anton Walbrook) and her jealous husband (Marius Goring) that, rather than choose between career and marriage, she kills herself. The sentimentality inherent in such a situation is alleviated by the abrupt harshness of the ending and the quality of the performances. But ultimately neither sentimentality nor the sometimes uneasy way in which art, fantasy and reality are melded together really matter. *The Red Shoes* is not so much a film as a cinematic experience and that is what makes it memorable.

MAIN CAST: Anton Walbrook, Moira Shearer, Marius Goring, Robert Helpmann, Albert Basserman, Frederick Ashton, Leonide Massine, Ludmilla Tcherina, Esmond Knight. DIR/PROD/SCR: Michael Powell, Emeric Pressburger; PHOT: Jack Cardiff; MUS: Brian Easdale; PROD DESIGN: Hein Heckroth.

OSCAR: Best art direction/set decoration (Heckroth, Arthur Lawson); Best music. OSCAR NOMINATIONS: Best film, best original story (Powell, Pressburger); best film editing (Reginald Mills). (Winner best film 1948: *Hamlet*.)

133 minutes. Colour

Moira Shearer in the first – and easily the best – of her half dozen or so movies.

La Règle du Jeu
The Rules of the Game (1939)

The potted history of Renoir's master-piece is as follows: it was initially greet-ed by howls of outrage, was withdrawn and hacked by thirty minutes, was banned as demoralising by the Vichy government and banned again as politi-cally dangerous by the Nazis. Then the master negative was destroyed in an air raid. It was not until 1956 that the film was painstakingly reconstructed and it was 1959 before the full, restored ver-sion was seen again (at the Venice festi-val). You feel it can only be due to someone in that Great Cutting Room in the Sky that the film survives at all to be included, as it regularly is, in peo-ple's lists of the all-time top ten. Loosely adapting Alfred de Musset's *Les Caprices de Marianne*, Renoir used a comedy of manners, mistaken identi-ty and sexual jealousy to make a per-sonal, ironic statement on the state of his nation after the farce of the Munich agreement. The setting is a weekend

The dissection of a beleaguered society which seeks to protect itself by laying down rules for everything.

party at a palatial country home. The protagonists belong to a decadent society which is already destroying itself from within but which, abiding by a particular set of rules, maintains the appearance of civilisation and is so intent on keeping up a solid front that it can even rationalise and absorb the shooting of one of the guests by a gamekeeper. In examining this rich and complex web of characters and relationships, Renoir – who exercised total control over the film and indeed played one of the pivotal roles himself – was also casting a critical and mocking eye on the moral state of France and its destructive class system as world war threatened. The superb result is so full of dangerous ideas it's little wonder the Nazis banned it.

MAIN CAST: Marcel Dalio, Nora Gregor, Roland Toutain, Jean Renoir, Mila Parély, Paulette Dubost, Gaston Modot, Julien Carette. DIR/PROD/SCR: Jean Renoir; PHOT: Jean Bachelet; MUS ARRANGER: Robert Desormières, Joseph Kosma.

OSCAR NOMINATIONS: None. (Winner best film 1939: *Gone with the Wind*.)

113 minutes. B&W. French – subtitled

Richard III (1956)

Laurence Olivier was the greatest actor I have ever seen or ever expect to see but on the whole his screen career was a disappointment. *Wuthering Heights, Rebecca, The Entertainer* – yes, fine. But there were too many films made, as he once slyly told me, 'not necessarily for artistic reasons', too many cameo roles and, towards the end, too many rank bad movies, so, for me at least, his glowing reputation in the cinema rests on the three adaptations of Shakespeare – *Henry V, Hamlet* and *Richard III*. (I exclude *Othello* because that was essentially a filmed stage pro-

duction.) Of these *Henry V* was the most spectacular and *Hamlet* the most successful (certainly in terms of Oscars), but *Richard III* was the one in which Olivier, the actor, was at his most commanding. His was the definitive Richard, a performance so outstanding that it deterred a couple of generations of actors from even essaying the part. You may argue, and I will not demur too strongly, that Olivier, the director, was some way below his best form, but his playing of Crookback gave us a portrayal of villainy that has yet to be matched. This

Olivier often said his interpretation of a character began with the nose – in Richard's case a bold and handsome nose.

is a monster (morally and physically) who is yet a man of wit and charm, a man who is both funny and ferocious, terrible and likeable, cruel and sexy. His courtship of Claire Bloom's Anne is dazzling in its lewdness and audacity. The battle scene may have been disappointing, the cutting of the text sometimes a shade infelicitous but Olivier's performance transcends all that.

MAIN CAST: Laurence Olivier, Claire Bloom, Ralph Richardson, John Gielgud, Cedric Hardwicke, Alec Clunes, Stanley Baker, Mary Kerridge, Pamela Brown, Norman Wooland. SCR: Laurence Olivier; PROD: Olivier, Alexander Korda; SCREEN ADAPTATION: Olivier, Alan Dent; PHOT: Otto Heller; MUS: William Walton.

OSCAR NOMINATION: Best actor (Olivier). (Winner best film 1956: *Around the World in 80 Days*.)

161 minutes. Colour

Schindler's List (1993)

Just when we thought that Steven Spielberg, brilliant though he is, might never make a truly adult movie he came up with this. During the Second World War Oskar Schindler, an Austrian businessman, saved the lives of countless Jews by persuading the Nazis to let them work in his factory rather than die in concentration camps. His motive initially was profit – this was a cheap labour force – but eventually sheer humanity: he wanted to save 'his Jews'. The story, based on a novel itself based firmly on fact, could easily have lent itself to sentimentality. Spielberg avoids that, just as, except towards the end, he avoids trying to explain the complex and probably inexplicable Schindler. This is a film of marvellous tension and horror, in which the enormity of the Holocaust – the more heartrending for being almost casually depicted – and the mindless cruelty of the Nazi prison camp commandant (Fiennes) speak vividly for themselves. The acting of Neeson, as Schindler, of Kingsley, as his Jewish accountant, and of Fiennes is faultless, but the true star of the film is the director, whose work, though superb, is admirably unobtrusive and always the servant, never the master, of his material. There is no preaching here, no editorial comment for none is needed.

After 20 years of producing box office hits with no Oscar recognition Spielberg's film took seven Academy Awards and all was forgiven.

This is a story that seems simply to unfold just as the events it chronicles must have done and therefore the actions of the Nazis seem all the more terrifying and appalling and those of Schindler the more amazing. The one eye-catching trick Spielberg permits himself – the recurring motif of a little girl in a red coat providing the only splash of colour – is splendidly vindicated because of all the victims in the film it is this girl, mostly seen only at a distance, whom you remember and grieve over most vividly.

MAIN CAST: Liam Neeson, Ben Kingsley, Ralph Fiennes, Caroline Goodall, Jonathan Sagalle, Embeth Davidz. DIR: Steven Spielberg; PROD: Spielberg, Gerald R. Molen, Branko Lustig; SCR: Steven Zaillian (from the novel by Thomas Keneally); PHOT: Janusz Kaminski; MUS: John Williams.

OSCARS: Best film; best director; best screenplay; best cinematography; best production design (Allan Starski); best editing (Michael Kahn); best music. OSCAR NOMINATIONS: Best actor (Neeson); best supporting actor (Fiennes); best costume design (Anna Biedrzycka-Sheppard); best make-up.

195 minutes. B&W

The Searchers (1956)

Simply the best western ever made. Admittedly it could be accused of lending respectability to the plethora of 'psychological' westerns that sprang up around the same time. But whereas most of those made the mistake of ascribing twentieth-century attitudes (especially towards the Indians) to nineteenth-century men, *The Searchers* retained an immaculate sense of time, place and character. John Wayne, an embittered Confederate veteran of the Civil War, and Jeffrey Hunter, a young half-breed, are the eponymous searchers, looking for a white girl abducted by the Comanches who had slaughtered her family. Hunter, her adoptive brother, wants to rescue her; Wayne wants to kill her because, in his view, she would already have suffered a fate infinitely worse than death – defloration by a savage. Wayne's hatred of the Indians is extreme but not, as it would appear today, insufferably racist because, as the film makes clear when the men repeatedly return to base during their five-year search, the Indians are the biggest threat to the settlers' dream of peace, security and home. Generally speaking, Ford was the cinematic poet of the West, its eulogist, but here he is in much grimmer mood. The wilderness (mostly represented by his beloved Monument Valley) has never been so bleak or menacing. There are no towns in *The Searchers*, merely outposts and lonely homesteads. This is hostile territory and, although the film contains less action than the traditional western, the elements, the vast landscape itself and the constant fear of attack by the Comanches help maintain an undercurrent of edgy tension. From the first memorable shot of Wayne framed in a doorway to the equally memorable – and almost identical – closer, *The Searchers* is a film of quite riveting power executed faultlessly by a director who had no peer as a maker of westerns.

MAIN CAST: John Wayne, Jeffrey Hunter, Natalie Wood, Vera Miles, Ward Bond, John Qualen, Henry Brandon, Harry Carey, jun., Dorothy Jordan. DIR: John Ford; PROD: Merian C. Cooper; SCR: Frank S. Nugent (from a novel by Alan le May); PHOT: Winton C. Hoch; MUS: Max Steiner.

OSCAR NOMINATIONS: None. (Winner best film 1956: *Around the World in 80 Days*.)

119 minutes. Colour

The searchers and the sought in the magnificent but threatening terrain of Monument Valley.

The Seven Samurai (1954)
Shichi-nin no Samurai

This was the film which, at the time, succeeded *Rashomon* as Kurosawa's acknowledged masterpiece, a genuine epic notable both for the simplicity of its plot and action and the complexity of the character development. In sixteenth-century Japan and in an age of upheaval and civil disorder, seven, as it were freelance, samurai warriors are employed by desperate villagers to pro-

tect them from the annual raid on their crops and produce by a group of bandits. This is the stuff of westerns and indeed it became a notable western in John Sturges's 1960 remake *The Magnificent Seven*. But what the American film lacked was the code and honour of the samurai – qualities unknown to the unemployed gunfight-

ers. By emphasising these things along with the Japanese caste system and thus revealing the paradox of samurai warriors fighting and dying for peasants, people whom normally they would treat with disdain, Kurosawa presented a story that was simultaneously familiar and alien. The climactic, rain-soaked, mud-spattered battle scene with the camera swooping and wheeling between samurai, peasants and bandits is brutally realistic and at times anticipates Sam Peckinpah's *The Wild Bunch* (1969) by showing the violence in slow motion. The overall blend of savagery and nobility, subtlety and broad humour makes what is essentially an action/adventure movie into something quite magnificent.

MAIN CAST: Takashi Shimura, Toshiro Mifune, Yoshio Onaba, Osao Kimura, Seiji Miyaguchi, Kuninori Kodo. DIR: Akira Kurosawa; PROD: Shojiro Motoki; SCR: Kurosawa, Shinobu Hashimoto, Hideo Oguni; PHOT: Asaichi Nakai; MUS: Fumio Hayasaka.

OSCAR NOMINATIONS (1956): Best art direction/set decoration (Takashi Matsuyama); best costumes (Kohei Ezaki). (Winner best film 1956: *Around the World in 80 Days*; winner best foreign language film: *La Strada*.)

208 minutes. B&W. Japanese – subtitled

Kurosawa acknowledges his debt to Hollywood. Hollywood took payment in full by cheekily reworking *The Seven Samurai.*

The Seventh Seal
Det Sjunde Inseglet (1957)

A medieval knight (Max von Sydow) returning to Sweden from the Crusades finds a land ravaged by the Black Death and hysteria. A demented monk has inspired a cult for self-flagellation; witches, blamed for the plague, are tortured and burnt. As he progresses through this horrifying, devastated country the knight treats each encounter as another step on his path

towards knowledge of God and His relationship with man. The classic centrepiece of the film (which takes its title from the Book of Revelations) is the game of chess which von Sydow plays with Death and which he uses to win himself a reprieve, to gain time wherein to come to terms with God and the remnants of his own faith. Over the whole of this sombre, brooding film there seems to hang the threat of an even greater disaster waiting to happen, the dreadful Day of Judgement itself. Clearly influenced by early religious paintings and filling his screen with astounding images of lust, beauty and cruelty, Bergman evoked a marvellous sense of period, of the hardship and squalor of medieval life. Yet there is an allegorical side to the story, too. The plague, the awful possibility of something worse, spoke clearly to a modern generation living in fear of the nuclear bomb. Despite the denouement, in which the knight tricks Death by sacrificing himself to save the two believers, the travelling player and his wife who are perhaps the only hopeful characters in the film, *The Seventh Seal* is a bleak vision of man's destiny, but so superbly and grippingly made that it instantly established its director's reputation as one of the most significant figures in world cinema.

MAIN CAST: Max von Sydow, Gunnar Bjornstrand, Bengt Ekerot, Nils Poppe, Bibi Andersson, Erik Strandmark, Gunnel Lindblom. DIR/SCR: Ingmar Bergman; PROD: Allan Ekelund; PHOT: Gunnar Fischer; MUS: Erik Nordgren.

OSCAR NOMINATIONS: None. (Winner best film 1957: *The Bridge on the River Kwai*; winner best foreign language film: *The Nights of Cabiria*.)

95 minutes. B&W. Swedish – subtitled

The first of two films (*Wild Strawberries* was the other) which, in one year, proved Bergman to be a master of the cinema.

Shane (1953)

Shane is a classic western, not only in content, but also in form and style. There is about it the kind of simplicity that is perfectly suited to the genre. In late nineteenth-century Wyoming the homesteaders are being harassed by the cattlemen. Now this is one of the two archetypal western plots. The first is about settlers threatened by Indians; this, the second, is about fences. The homesteaders want them; the cattlemen don't. The symbolism is obvious

because the fences mean that 'them days is over'. With the land divided neatly into individual farms and ranches, the wild era will have passed, the West will have been tamed. Shane (Alan Ladd), a gunman who wishes to settle down, throws in his lot with the homesteaders, in particular Van Heflin, his wife, Jean Arthur, and son, Brandon de Wilde. Shane is tired of violence and wants no more of it, but, goaded by the cattlemen's hired guns (notably Jack Palance), he is forced into the inevitable showdown. A hundred other westerns have told a similar tale but none so well as *Shane*. The action, when it finally comes, is of course crucial, but so too are the development of relationships and atmosphere: the effect of Shane on the farmer, whom he inspires to stand up for himself, on the wife, who is disturbingly attracted to him, and on the boy, who admires him; and the character of Shane, who, no matter how strong his desire to change and put down roots, will always be a loner and a nomad. The casting was just about faultless and Alan Ladd, who was not generally renowned for the excellence of his acting, could hardly have been better.

MAIN CAST: Alan Ladd, Van Heflin, Jean Arthur, Jack Palance, Brandon de Wilde, Ben Johnson, Edgar Buchanan, Elisha Cooke, jun., Emile Meyer. DIR: George Stevens; PROD: Stevens, Ivan Moffat; SCR: A.B. Guthrie, jun. (from the novel by Jack Schaefer); PHOT: Loyal Griggs; MUS: Victor Young.

OSCAR: Best cinematography. OSCAR NOMINATIONS: Best film; best director; best supporting actor (Palance, de Wilde); best screenplay. (Winner best film 1953: *From Here to Eternity*.)

118 minutes. Colour

Alan Ladd, an unlikely hero, thows in his lot with the homesteaders

Singin' In The Rain (1952)

(Debbie Reynolds) is recruited to do the talking for her. The complications (Hagen thinks she and Kelly are in love; Kelly thinks they're not) and the solutions are delightfully worked out and the performances (that of Hagen in particular) are splendid. But it's the musical numbers (even the ballet featuring Cyd Charisse, which has nothing whatsoever to do with the rest of the film) that are unforgettable. Two of the routines indeed – Kelly in the title sequence and Donald O'Connor's remarkable rendition of 'Make 'em Laugh' – are unequalled anywhere else. O'Connor, here in his best role, was as athletic and talented a dancer as Kelly himself; it was his misfortune to appear on the scene just as the musical was beginning to fade out as a staple ingredient of Hollywood fare.

MAIN CAST: Gene Kelly, Donald O'Connor, Debbie Reynolds, Jean Hagen, Millard Mitchell, Cyd Charisse, Rita Moreno, Douglas Fowley. DIR: Stanley Donen, Gene Kelly; PROD: Arthur Freed; SCR: Arthur Green, Betty Comden; PHOT: Harold Rosson; MUS: Nacio Herb Brown; LYR: Freed; CHOR: Kelly; MUS DIR: Lennie Hayton.

OSCAR NOMINATIONS: Best supporting actress (Hagen); best musical direction. (Winner best film 1952: *The Greatest Show on Earth*.)

102 minutes. Colour

The greatest of all musicals, a joyful, fast-moving romp of a romantic comedy which looks both nostalgically and satirically at the earlier days of Hollywood. A major film studio is making the transition from silent movies to sound and the worrying question is: can its two leading box-office stars, Gene Kelly and Jean Hagen, cope with these new-fangled talkies? Kelly's okay (given a few elocution lessons) but, alas, Hagen has a voice like a wood saw cutting through concrete. So a young singer and actress

Everyone's favourite musical? Pretty nearly. And the title sequence is certainly one of the most famous in cinematic history.

Sleeper (1973)

The most evenly constructed as well as the last (so far, anyway) of Woody Allen's pure comedies. But beyond all that, in its rapid pace and assured handling of farce it is almost a latterday equivalent of the great slapstick comedies of the silent era. The influence of Chaplin, Keaton, Harold Lloyd and many more of Allen's comic icons can be seen in sequence after sequence. But Allen is neither a mimic nor a thief. He will borrow, certainly, but what he borrows he develops, adapts and builds upon. And to that he adds his own matchless gift for the one-liner. In *Sleeper* he plays a meek, late-twentieth-century vegetarian, a man who, as he says, is 'beaten up by Quakers' and who spends 200 years in suspended animation after a not entirely successful operation to remove a stomach ulcer. When he is revived he finds himself in a police state, reluctantly joins a band of rebels seeking to overthrow the ruling tyrant, escapes from a police raid, disguises himself as a robot domestic servant, encounters a pretentious and deeply untalented poet (Diane Keaton), is captured and brainwashed by the state police and so on. There is ample scope in all this for satire on the future, the present and the immediate past and Allen takes full advantage of it. (Of President Nixon, for example, he says they counted the spoons every time he left the White House.) If hitherto there had been doubt that Allen was America's most talented comic actor/writer/director there was none after *Sleeper*. Later he earned solemn critical respect with films of deeper import but, good as they were, none has so far been as consistently funny or as close to simple, classical comedy as *Sleeper*.

MAIN CAST: Woody Allen, Diane Keaton, John Beck, Mary Gregory. DIR: Woody Allen; PROD: Jack Rollins, Charles Joffe; SCR: Allen, Marshall Brickman; PHOT: David M. Walsh; MUS: Allen.

OSCAR NOMINATIONS: None. (Winner best film 1973: *The Sting*.)

88 minutes. Colour

Allen as incompetent domestic robot and
(above) with Keaton, the even less compe-
tent poet.

Some Like It Hot (1959)

The basic plot, superbly exploited by cast, writers and director alike, is enough on its own to sustain a first-rate, full-length comedy-thriller. Two out-of-work musicians (Jack Lemmon and Tony Curtis) inadvertently witness the St Valentine's Day Massacre and, to escape the pursuing gangsters, disguise themselves as women and join an all-girl band. But to this already ingenious

Once, after she had fluffed numerous takes, Wilder took Monroe aside and said, 'Marilyn, don't worry.' And she said, 'Worry about what?'

blend of slapstick and sophistication is added a wickedly sharp examination of gender and sexual identity. Curtis promptly falls in love with fellow band member Marilyn Monroe (as deliciously awkward, vulnerable and desirable as only she could be) and seethes with frustration because, the way things are, he can't declare his passion. Lemmon meanwhile, totally beguiled by his own image of himself as a sexy woman, is being wooed by a millionaire, Joe E. Brown. It's Brown who, finally learning that Lemmon is a man, provides one of the cinema's great lines. 'Nobody's perfect,' he says contentedly – and still besottedly. For its time (before the permissiveness of the 1960s) this was very spicy stuff – too spicy certainly for those notorious conservatives, the Oscar voters, though not for audiences either then or now. The Brown/Lemmon relationship may no longer have much shock effect, but the

wit, speed and zest of the movie lose nothing with the passing of time. During the making of the film Monroe was at her most difficult and tiresome ('Kissing her,' said Curtis 'was like kissing Hitler.') But the result – a performance of melting charm – was worth it.

MAIN CAST: Jack Lemmon, Tony Curtis, Marilyn Monroe, Joe E. Brown, George Raft, Pat O'Brien, Nehemiah Persoff, Mike Mazurki, George E. Stone, Joan Shawlee. DIR/PROD: Billy Wilder; SCR: Wilder, I.A.L. Diamond; PHOT: Charles Lang, jun.; MUS: Adolph Deutsch.

OSCAR: Best costume design (Orry-Kelly). OSCAR NOMINATIONS: Best actor (Lemmon); best director; best screenplay; best cinematography; best art direction/set decoration (Ted Haworth, Edward G. Boyle). (Winner best film 1959: *Ben-Hur*.)

122 minutes. B&W

Stagecoach (1939)

Stagecoach was the film that gave the western respectability. Since 1931 when *Cimarron* had become the first (and still the only) western to win the Oscar for best film, the genre had fallen into disrepute. Vast numbers of horse operas had been turned out, but mostly they were low-budget quickies, programme fillers purveying nothing more than simplistic action. But *Stagecoach*, based on a novel which was itself inspired by de Maupassant's *Boule de Suif*, proved that this kind of film could deal in relationships and conflict, fact and fable, grandeur and poetry as well as any other. The tension inside the stagecoach where a number of small human dramas are played out is heightened by the increasing danger of an attack by Indians which, when it comes, provides as exciting and satisfying a climax as you could wish. Beyond all that there is the burgeoning romance between the prostitute, shunned by her fellow passengers, and the outlaw, the Ringo Kid, who alone treats her like a lady. Marlene Dietrich and Gary Cooper were originally cast in these roles; it was John Ford, making his first western in thirteen years, who insisted on replacing them with Claire Trevor and John Wayne. This was an inspired choice. Dietrich and Cooper, both already well established, would have been too top-heavy with glamour for a film in which the story itself was the star. By contrast Trevor had been in only six movies and was more or less unknown, as was Wayne, who in eleven years of earnest endeavour and more than sixty perfectly forgettable pictures had made very little impact. After *Stagecoach*, of course, his career was rather different. The film was remade for the cinema in 1966 and for TV in 1986. By comparison with the original both these efforts were pathetic.

The western achieving artistic respectability; Wayne achieving overnight stardom after more than ten years and sixty-two forgettable movies.

MAIN CAST: John Wayne, Claire Trevor, Thomas Mitchell, John Carradine, Donald Meek, George Bancroft, Andy Devine, Berton Churchill, Louise Platt. DIR: John Ford; PROD: Walter Wanger; SCR: Dudley Nicholls (from *Stage to Lordsburg* by Ernest Haycox); PHOT: Bert Glennon, Ray Binger; MUS: Richard Hageman, Frank Harling, John Leopold, Leo Shuken.

OSCARS: Best supporting actor (Mitchell); best music. OSCAR NOMINATIONS: Best film; best director; best cinematography; best art direction (Alexander Toluboff); best film editing (Otho Lovering, Dorothy Spencer). (Winner best film 1949: *Gone with the Wind.*)

La Strada (1954)

The fact that this, Fellini's fourth
film, has won more than fifty awards
in various parts of the world is not,
in itself, a guarantee of excellence;
but at least it indicates the strong
universal appeal of the story and the

stunning impact the picture makes. In the end it is perhaps the style, quite as much as the substance, that exercises the imagination. It begins as neorealism and moves gradually into romanticism as we follow the bizarre – as ever with Fellini – adventures of Giulietta Masina, a naïve, almost simple, girl who is sold by her poverty-stricken mother to an itinerant strongman

(Anthony Quinn). During their travels they join a circus where she becomes friendly with a tightrope walker (Richard Basehart), the antithesis to the brutish Quinn. Both the travelling and the circus represent Fellini's sardonic view of what life is about and the characters are equally symbolic. Masina is innocence, Quinn brute strength and power, Basehart the artist. A marvellous scene in which, in the dark, Basehart talks to the girl about the stars typifies the way in which Fellini can blend reality and fantasy so that they are almost indistinguishable. In a film often overlaid with pessimism and sentimentality, the director expounds his belief that life can be cruel and harsh, lonely and comic, but also that everyone has a place, a purpose. The mood of the picture, the observation, the attention to detail and the acting are deeply impressive. Basehart is very good indeed, while Masina's portrayal of the waif has evoked quite startling comparisons with practically everyone from Chaplin to Stan Laurel and from Harpo Marx to Marcel Marceau. Such praise is no doubt extravagant but only just, for this is an extraordinary performance.

MAIN CAST: Giulietta Masina, Richard Basehart, Anthony Quinn. DIR: Federico Fellini; PROD: Carlo Ponti, Dino de Laurentiis; SCR: Fellini, Ennio Flaiano, Tullio Pinelli; PHOT: Otello Martelli; MUS: Nino Rota.

OSCAR (1956): Best foreign language film. OSCAR NOMINATION: Best screenplay. (Winner best film 1956: *Around the World in 80 Days*.)

115 minutes. B&W. Italian – subtitled

Fellini of the earlier, more classical, period – before flamboyance and self-indulgence invaded his work.

Sunset Boulevard (1950)

Quite the blackest and most cynical of Hollywood's attacks upon itself and very possibly Billy Wilder's best film. The story, told in flashback by a corpse floating face down in a Beverly Hills swimming pool, is more than merely a bleak satire on the film industry. In its study of ambition and humiliation, of the lengths to which a young man will go to make his way in the world and to which an older woman will go to hang on to the young man in her life it has a far wider application. This is in fact a very cruel film, not only in its coldly unsentimental look at the workings of Hollywood but in its actual casting. Gloria Swanson plays a once-great star destroyed by the coming of sound; Erich von Stroheim a once-great director now reduced to acting as her chauffeur. The parallels with their own lives are sharply pointed up by the fact that

Swanson is seen watching *Queen Kelly*, Stroheim's unfinished potential masterpiece in which she starred and which virtually ruined both their careers. William Holden is the writer (and narrator) who hides from his creditors in Swanson's house and stays to become her lover, her dependant, the writer of the script with which she hopes to make her comeback, and finally her victim. This was the last film on which Wilder collaborated with Charles Brackett. Their partnership ended in some acrimony because Wilder insisted on turning what Brackett had conceived as a light-hearted comedy into the dark, maliciously witty picture it became.

Gloria Swanson – 'ready for my close-up, Mr de Mille' and 'sleepwalking along the giddy heights of a lost career'.

MAIN CAST: Gloria Swanson, William Holden, Erich von Stroheim, Fred Clark, Nancy Olson, Jack Webb, Cecil B. de Mille, Lloyd Gough, H.B. Warner, Buster Keaton. DIR: Billy Wilder; PROD: Charles Brackett; SCR: Wilder, Brackett, D.M. Marshman, jun.; PHOT: John F. Seitz; MUS: Franz Waxman.

OSCARS: Best screenplay; best art direction/set decoration (Hans Dreier, John Meehan, Sam Comer, Ray Moyer); best music. OSCAR NOMINATIONS: Best film; best actor (Holden); best actress (Swanson); best director; best supporting actor (von Stroheim); best supporting actress (Olson); best cinematography; best film editing (Arthur Schmidt, Doane Harrison). (Winner best film 1950: *All Above Eve*.)

110 minutes. B&W

Taxi Driver (1976)

Taxi Driver is the story of Travis Bickle, a profoundly disturbed Vietnam veteran (superbly played by Robert De Niro) who is so appalled by the dirt and moral decay that he sees all round him as he drives his cab through New York that he embarks on a murderous one-man campaign to clean up the streets. The focus of his madness is a 12-year-old prostitute (Jodie Foster); and because the victims of his rampage are her pimp (Harvey Keitel) and similar examples of urban lowlife, he becomes a folk hero. We learn nothing much about Bickle except that he is an ex-Marine and a man seething with frustration at being in a city full of women he wants but cannot have (Cybill Shepherd especially) and men, quite unsuitable men, who can have them. This is not at all a heroic figure; he is in many ways repellent. And yet we are on his side to the extent that, seeing the city through his eyes, we share his disgust at its corruption and filth and his vision of it as a kind of

De Niro – unlikely cabby, unlikely folk hero; and Foster – the child for hire.

hell on earth. *Taxi Driver* is a brilliantly made film with images vivid and horrifying enough to sear the mind. Those audiences who cheered Bickle on as he embarked on his rampage were missing the point. This is not a *Death Wish*, a simplistic story about a vigilante; it is rather an indictment of the way society is composed, the way it behaves. If it seemed apposite in 1976 you only have to look at what is happening in the inner cities to see that it is even more so now.

MAIN CAST: Robert De Niro, Jodie Foster, Cybill Shepherd, Peter Boyle, Harvey Keitel, Leonard Harris. DIR: Martin Scorsese; PROD: Michael and Julia Phillips; SCR: Paul Schrader; PHOT: Michael Chapman; MUS: Bernard Herrmann.

OSCAR NOMINATIONS: Best film; best actor (De Niro); best supporting actress (Foster); best music. (Winner best film 1976: *Rocky*.)

113 minutes. Colour

The Thief Of Bagdad (1940)

The silent 1924 movie of the same name starring Douglas Fairbanks, sen., was hailed as 'a work of rare genius'. Possibly it was for its time. But this one is even better, even more magical and enchanting, even closer to capturing the spirit of the *Arabian Nights* on film. Sabu is the boy thief, John Justin the blinded prince whom he befriends, Conrad Veidt the evil Grand Vizier who has stolen the prince's kingdom. June Duprez is the heroine and – best of all – Rex Ingram plays the vast, jovial but terrifying genie of the bottle. This is a thoroughly enjoyable, sump-tuous and beautifully photographed movie with special effects – especially the magic carpet and the flying horse – that are spectacular even today. Again it's an example of how occasionally and against all the odds a film can work wonderfully. This one was begun at Denham Studios in 1939. Then war broke out, plans to shoot in Baghdad had, perforce, to be abandoned and the production moved to Hollywood. In the end Baghdad was built in the Mojave desert. Meanwhile, the direct-ors changed almost by the day. Apart from the three who are credited, three

The genie, the wicked vizier, the blind prince and the boy thief – the magic of the *Arabian Nights* made celluloid.

others – Alexander and Zoltan Korda and William Cameron Menzies – also contributed bits and pieces. But somehow it all came seamlessly and delightfully together. Two later versions were made – one, starring Steve Reeves, in Italy in 1960; the second, a television movie with Peter Ustinov and Terence Stamp, in Europe in 1978. Neither matched up in any way to the 1940 production.

MAIN CAST: Conrad Veidt, Sabu, John Justin, Rex Ingram, June Duprez, Miles Malleson, Mary Morris, Morton Selten. DIR: Michael Powell, Ludwig Berger, Tim Whelan; PROD: Alexander Korda; SCR: Miles Malleson, Lajos Biro; PHOT: Georges Périnal, Osmond Borradaile; MUS: Miklos Rozsa.

OSCARS: Best cinematography; best art direction (Vincent Korda); best special effects (Lawrence Butler, Jack Whitney). OSCAR NOMINATION: Best music. (Winner best film 1940: *Rebecca*.)

106 minutes. Colour

The Third Man (1949)

On the face of it *The Third Man*
should simply have come and gone,
remembered – if at all – as simply
another postwar thriller. The basic
theme of a man seeking an old friend,
first to be told he is dead, then to learn
that he is still alive, had been used as
recently as 1944 in the film of Eric
Ambler's *The Mask of Dimitrios*; the
protagonist (Joseph Cotten as the
writer Holly Martins) is less interesting
than the supporting characters; and
there's an unhappy ending. And yet
from this potentially unpromising
material came an abiding classic. The
indefinable cinematic alchemy that can,
just occasionally, turn brass into gold
ensured that everything was precisely
right – the direction, the writing, the
cinematography, the acting, the
inspired use of Anton Karas's zither
music and, above all, Orson Welles's
stunning performance as Harry Lime,
the friend who is not dead but has
become a racketeer preying on the sick.
His first, belated, appearance in a dark-
ened doorway, his sardonic, mocking
grin suddenly illuminated as a light
goes on in a nearby apartment is one of
the great moments of the cinema. Set
against the corruption and desperation
of postwar Vienna, Welles's study of a
witty, intelligent man who had deliberately chosen evil is, I think, the best
performance he ever gave. But then
everyone else involved was also in
prime, mid-season form. *The Third
Man* is fresh each time you see it – a
film that has no sell-by date.

**Holly Martins, the amateur sleuth, learn-
ing – as Harry Lime tells him – that 'the
world doesn't make any heroes.'**

MAIN CAST: Joseph Cotten, Trevor Howard, Orson Welles, Alida Valli, Bernard Lee, Wilfrid Hyde-White. DIR: Carol Reed; PROD: Reed, Alexander Korda, David O. Selznick; SCR: Graham Greene; PHOT: Robert Krasker; MUS: Anton Karas.

OSCAR (1950): Best cinematography. OSCAR NOMINATIONS: Best director; best film editing (Oswald Hafenrichter). (Winner best film 1950: *All About Eve*.)

104 minutes. B&W

The Thirty-Nine Steps (1935)

Hitchcock fastened on to John Buchan's novel, discarded most of it except the title and around what remained concocted a classic comedy-thriller of his own. Here Richard

Hannay (Robert Donat) has been in Canada, not South Africa; he gives shelter to a spy and, when she is murdered, takes on her mission with the patriotic motive of stopping the sale of

vital military secrets to an unnamed enemy. The basic plot – Hanney, himself suspected of the murder, falling into the hands of the gang he seeks to unmask and being at various times both fugitive and captive – could have come straight from some penny-dreadful. But Hitchcock's imagination and sly wit, the exciting pace and the understated but crackling sexuality between Donat and Madeleine Carroll when they are handcuffed together give the film a vivacity that never fades. Hitchcock always maintained that the sexiest women were the apparently cool Nordic blondes and from Carroll he brought forth a performance to prove it. Donat is exactly right as the unflappable hero, the young Peggy Ashcroft is memorable as the crofter's wife who helps Hannay escape from the police and there's a satisfying neat-

ness in the way the picture begins and ends at a music hall. It's a considerable tribute to Hitchcock that both subsequent versions of *The Thirty-Nine Steps* (in 1959 and 1978) owe far more to him than they do to Buchan.

MAIN CAST: Robert Donat, Madeleine Carroll, Godfrey Tearle, Lucie Mannheim, Peggy Ashcroft, John Laurie, Wylie Watson, Helen Haye. DIR: Alfred Hitchcock; PROD: Ivor Montague; SCR: Charles Bennett, Alma Reville (from the novel by John Buchan); PHOT: Bernard Knowles; MUS: Hubert Bath, Jack Beaver.

OSCAR NOMINATIONS: None. (Winner best film 1935: *Mutiny on the Bounty*.)

87 minutes. B&W

Bondage with sexuality but no sex. Donat and Carroll handcuffed, in bed, but chaste to the end.

Three Colours Red (1994)

Or, to put it another way, *Three Colours Red, White* and *Blue* because you can't really separate the respective parts of Kieslowski's trilogy. Well, you can, since they all tell different stories but they are inextricably linked by the colours of the French flag and the revolutionary ideals represented therein – liberty, fraternity, equality – plus, most importantly, the style and vision of the director. The first film, *Blue*, is set in Paris and explores individual freedom in the modern age; *White*, which moves from Paris to Poland, examines the notion of equality. And *Red*, set in Geneva and centering on the strange but compelling friendship which springs up between a model (Jacob) and a reclusive, eavesdropping judge (Trintignant) after she has accidentally run over his dog and brings it back to

him, represents fraternity and, like its predecessors, a lot more than that. Between them the three films delicately touch on almost every aspect of the human condition. Each segment can be seen, appreciated and perfectly understood on its own, though for once the whole is greater than the parts because together they add up to a remarkable cinematic achievement. *Red*, which, in a curious and dramatic final sequence, ties all the themes together and reintroduces some of the characters from the earlier films, is the richest and most complex of the three. The relationship between the warm-hearted young model and the judge who, Godlike, sits alone in his home tapping into other people's telephone conversations, develops naturally from its unlikely beginning to something totally cred-

Three Colours Red: **the best part of Koslowski's trilogy.**

ible. Although Kieslowski, with his masterly use of composition, colour, camera angles and, not least, his actors, is clearly the driving force behind the whole enterprise, much credit must also go to Piesiwicz, who was his co-writer on all three films.

MAIN CAST: Irene Jacob, Jean-Louis Trintignant, Frederique Feder, Jean-Pierre Lorit, Juliette Binoche, Julie Delpy, Benoit Regent, Zbigniew Zamachowski. DIR: Krzysztof Kieslowski; PROD: Marin Karmitz; PHOT: Piotr Sobocinski; MUS: Zbigniew Preisner.

OSCAR NOMINATIONS: Best director; best screenplay; best cinematography. (Winner best film 1994: *Forrest Gump.*)

99 minutes. Colour

To Be Or Not To Be (1942)

If this is not already on everybody's list
of the ten best comedies ever made
there is something seriously wrong
with the list. *To Be or Not to Be* is
hilariously funny; it is also daring and
even outrageous. The setting is Warsaw
during the Nazi occupation in the
Second World War; the protagonists
are Jack Benny as an actor-manager
whose vanity far outstrips his talent
and Carole Lombard as his flighty
actress wife. (This was Lombard's last
film. Two weeks after completing it she
was killed in an air crash while on a
tour to sell war bonds). The German
invasion has just about put the theatre
out of business but the thespians exact
glorious revenge when they join the
Polish underground and, putting their
skills to the ultimate test, create considerable havoc by impersonating leading Nazis – most notably Hitler. When
the film was first shown Lubitsch was
greatly castigated for his 'bad taste',
the moment that created most indignation coming when a German says of
Benny's performance as Hamlet: 'What
he did to Shakespeare, we are now
doing to Poland.' But to seize on that
was to overlook the most interesting
point: that the movie was using the
most potent form of propaganda –
ridicule – to cut the Western democra-
cies' enemies down to size. It used it to
such effect that the comedy still works
perfectly fifty years after it was made.
Indeed it is so splendidly funny that
Mel Brooks was unwise enough to
remake it in 1983. That the Brooks
version was universally regarded as a
disappointment had nothing to do
with the topicality – or lack of it – of

the story; it had everything to do with
the fact that Brooks, though a very
funny man and a master of bad taste
himself, is no Lubitsch.

MAIN CAST: Jack Benny, Carole Lombard, Robert Stack, Stanley Ridges, Felix Bressart, Sig Rumann, Lionel Atwill, Tom Dugan. DIR: Ernst Lubitsch; PROD: Lubitsch, Alexander Korda; SCR: Edwin Justus Mayer (from a story by Lubitsch and Melchior Lengyel); PHOT: Rudolph Maté; MUS: Werner Heymann.

OSCAR NOMINATION: Best music. (Winner best film 1942: *Mrs Miniver*.)

99 minutes. B&W

Tom Dugan as Hitler – or bad taste raised to an art form.

Top Hat (1935)

In his earlier incarnation as a film critic Graham Greene, reviewing *Top Hat*, described Fred Astaire as 'the nearest approach we are ever likely to have to a human Mickey Mouse ... He belongs to a fantasy world almost as free as Mickey's from the law of gravity ...' This is a far more accurate and perceptive assessment than that delivered by the casting director who, after seeing Astaire's first Hollywood screen test, remarked: 'Can't act. Slightly bald. Can dance a little' – and turned him down. Graham Greene, while greatly admiring Astaire, did not much like *Top Hat* but time has proved him wrong. This is now generally regarded as the best, lightest and frothiest of the Astaire-Ginger Rogers musicals. The usual slender plot (romantic complications, not unlike those in *The Gay Divorcee*, mistaken identity, the action switching from London to Venice) is unimportant. What matters is that with the aid of Irving Berlin's songs ('Top Hat' and 'Cheek to Cheek' among them) and Hermes Pan's choreography, Astaire and Rogers were never better together – which is another way of saying that they were twice as good as any other dance team has ever been. *Top Hat* is not perhaps a great musical, though it's delightfully played by a supporting cast of skilled *farceurs*. But Astaire, certainly, was touched with greatness and here especially he showed it.

MAIN CAST: Fred Astaire, Ginger Rogers, Edward Everett Horton, Helen Broderick, Eric Blore, Erik Rhodes. DIR: Mark Sandrich; PROD: Pandro S. Berman; SCR: Dwight Taylor, Allan Scott (from a play by Alexander Farago and Aladar Laszlo); PHOT: David Abel, Vernon Walker; MUS/LYR: Irving Berlin; CHOR: Hermes Pan.

OSCAR NOMINATIONS: Best film; best art direction (Carroll Clark, Van Nest Polglase); best song ('Cheek to Cheek'); best dance direction (Pan). (Winner best film 1935: *Mutiny on the Bounty*.)

100 minutes. B&W

The Treasure Of The Sierra Madre (1948)

This was accounted a flop when it first appeared. Audiences wanted the Bogart of *Casablanca*, not this avaricious, unsympathetic gold prospector forever muttering to himself. What they expected was Bogart, the movie star; what they got was Bogart, the actor, giving possibly the best performance of his life. They might also have been disappointed by the fact that a film set in the outdoors was too obviously studio-bound. But while more location shooting would certainly have improved the look of the picture, it could hardly have made it more powerful. The story tells of three ill-matched prospectors –

the elderly, experienced and toothless Walter Huston, the honest, straightforward young Tim Holt and the untrustworthy and finally deranged Bogart. They seek gold, find it and then, through greed, lose it. It's a study of character development (and, in Bogart's case, disintegration) as the two younger men begin to realise what Huston had known all along – that looking for gold is not a get-rich-quick business; that it takes hard work and patience. What they also learn is that finding the gold is only half the problem. The other half is keeping it and, as suspicion grows, worrying whether your partners will allow you to hold on to your share. The climactic scene in which bandits, led by Alfonso Bedoya, kill Bogart for his boots and mule, while the gold dust is caught up by the wind and blown God knows where should be included in any compilation of Great Moments from the Movies. This was the only film in which Walter Huston (who died three years later) was directed by his son, John. Both won Oscars. In 1985 John Huston directed his daughter Anjelica in *Prizzi's Honor* but this time, though again father and offspring were each nominated, only Anjelica won.

MAIN CAST: Humphrey Bogart, Walter Huston, Tim Holt, Alfonso Bedoya, Bruce Bennett, Barton MacLane, John Huston. DIR/SCR: John Huston (from the novel by B. Traven); PROD: Henry Blanke; PHOT: Ted McCord; MUS: Max Steiner.

OSCARS: Best director; best supporting actor (Walter Huston); best screenplay. OSCAR NOMINATION: Best film. (Winner best film 1948: *Hamlet*.)

126 minutes. B&W

'Fred C. Dobbs don't say nuthin' he don't mean' – Bogart, proving himself a liar from the start.

2001: A Space Odyssey (1968)

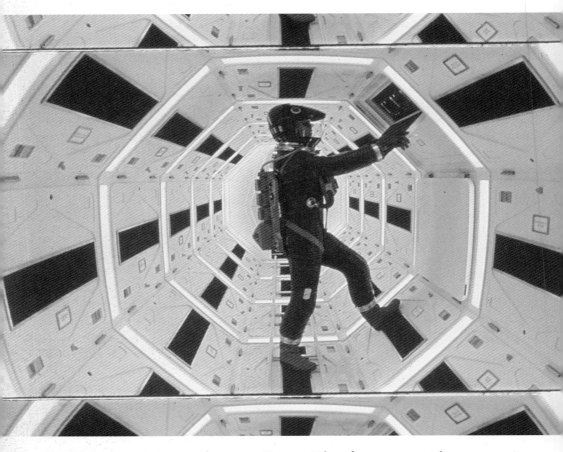

The universe is greater than man. No argument with that. But what Kubrick seems to be saying is that man's technology is also greater than man himself. The machines are the protagonists here, not the humans who occupy them. The strongest character is a robot, HAL 9000, which (or, as you come to believe, who) controls and manipulates the people inside the space ship. It has been suggested – not without reason – that *2001* is a cold obscure film as it traces man's development, both past and future, from caveman to rebirth on some higher astral plane.

What, for instance, is the true meaning of that curious monolith which crops up first on Earth, then on the Moon and is later found floating in space somewhere near Jupiter? Yet the mystery and the very obscurity merely add to the overall effect of a picture that used special effects more breathtakingly than they had ever been used before. This was perhaps not the first film to treat space travel seriously, nor the first to ponder the meaning of life and the existence (or otherwise) of some Supreme Being. But it was, I suggest, the first to tackle both subjects together and to discuss them on an intellectual, rather than a melodramatic, level. Since 1968 the development of special effects has been startling; too often nowadays the FX are the film. Ironically, that accusation was also levelled at *2001*, wrongly in my view. *2001* is so imaginative, breaks such new ground and remains, even now, so infuriatingly thought-provoking that it stands out as a landmark in the evolution of the cinema. One word of warning: **do not watch it on TV.** Television diminishes, shrivels, it. It must be seen in the cinema and on a big screen. (In 1984 Peter Hyams directed a sequel of sorts called *2010*. Not good and known to Kubrick fans as 'Ten Past Eight'.)

MAIN CAST: Keir Dullea, Gary Lockwood, William Sylvester, Daniel Richter, Douglas Rain (voice of HAL 9000), Leonard Rossiter, Margaret Tyzack, Robert Beatty. DIR: Stanley Kubrick; PROD: Kubrick, Victor Lyndon; SCR: Kubrick, Arthur C. Clarke (from Clarke's *The Sentinel*); PHOT: Geoffrey Unsworth, John Alcott; MUS: various classics.

OSCAR: Best special effects (Wally Veevers, Douglas Trumbull). OSCAR NOMINATIONS: Best director; best screenplay; best art direction/set decoration (Tony Masters, Harry Lange, Ernie Archer). (Winner best film 1968: *Oliver!*)

160 minutes (later cut by Kubrick to 141 minutes). Colour

Almost in a sense a space oddity in that it showed, very early, how potent brilliant special effects could be.

Unforgiven (1992)

At first glance a traditional western, a tale of revenge and money. An ageing, retired gunfighter (Eastwood) and his partners (Freeman and Woolvett) seek to earn the bounty on the heads of two cowboys who slashed a prostitute's face. Their quest takes them to a Wyoming town run by a sheriff (Hackman) who not only dispenses the law but is the law. In a way Eastwood and Hackman are two sides of the same coin – each ruthless, brutal when necessary, but each seeking a quieter life. Eastwood had retired into domesticity but now needs money to support his motherless children; Hackman bans guns from his town and savagely clamps down on any violence other than his own. How it all works out, who dies and who doesn't, is riveting enough but the subtext of the film is even more gripping. This is the old West revisited, the obverse side of John Ford's lyrical image. Eastwood's gunfighter is the hero but he's not a good man; in the past he has killed women and children as well as bad guys; and the world he and the others inhabit is the opposite of romantic – it's tough, dark, dirty, full of hardship, suffering and three-dimensional characters. You may not like all, or any, of those dimensions but they are there. And most unusually for a movie, western or otherwise, this film knows the importance of death. Here it's not just something that happens and is lightly forgotten as the plot moves on. Instead we get some inkling of what it must be like to kill someone, of the effect it has both on the killer and the people around him. As actor and director

Eastwood has made many fine films but *Unforgiven* is his masterpiece. When it first appeared people thought it might revive the western but it didn't. Because how today could you compete with it?

MAIN CAST: Clint Eastwood, Gene Hackman, Morgan Freeman, Jaimz Woolvett, Richard Harris, Frances Fisher, Saul Rubinek. DIR/PROD: Clint Eastwood; SCR: David Webb Peoples; PHOT: Jack N. Green; MUS: Lennie Niehaus.

OSCARS: Best picture; best director; best supporting actor (Hackman); best editor (Joel Cox). OSCAR NOMINATION: Best actor (Eastwood); best production design (Henry Bumstead); best photography; best screenplay; best sound.

131 minutes. Colour

Clint goes back to his roots in this cerebral Oscar-winning western.

Whisky Galore (1948)

The inspiration for the film was Compton Mackenzie's novel, the inspiration for the novel was the worst crisis that could possibly befall a Scottish community – a total whisky famine. This actually occurred during the Second World War on an island in the Outer Hebrides. The film examines affectionately and hilariously what might ensue in such circumstances if a ship carrying 50,000 cases of Scotch were to founder just offshore. And indeed that is exactly what did happen off the Isle of Eriskay, though in that case nobody knows how much of the precious cargo was rescued. In the movie, of course, the inhabitants of Todday, totally disregarding the law, salvage the whisky for themselves and devise the most ingenious schemes to hide it from authority, such as the Customs and Excise people and the English Home Guard commander (Basil Radford). This was Alexander Mackendrick's first film as a director for Ealing and it immediately took its

The unspeakable (Basil Radford, far left) in pursuit of the sublimely drinkable, here seen being drunk (below, right) by James Robertson Justice.

place among that studio's pantheon of screen classics. Much of the tension in the story comes from the islanders' efforts (ultimately successful) to outwit the sternly law-abiding Radford. And it's possible that the dramatic tension which gave the film an appealingly sharp edge came, as George Perry suggests in his book *Forever Ealing*, from the conflict between the Calvinist Mackendrick, whose sympathies lay with Radford, and his Russian-Jewish producer, Monja Danischewsky, who sided with the islanders. Their battle, if such it was, ended in a draw: the islanders got away with the whisky but, as the epilogue tells us, it didn't last long and everybody lived unhappily ever after. Mind you, that footnote probably owed a good deal to the moral code of the time, which insisted that crime (such as hanging on to salvaged whisky) must not be seen to pay and should therefore not be taken too seriously.

MAIN CAST: Basil Radford, Joan Greenwood, James Robertson Justice, Jean Cadell, Gordon Jackson, Wylie Watson, John Gregson, Catherine Lacey, Bruce Seton, Duncan Macrae, Compton Mackenzie, A.E. Matthews. DIR: Alexander Mackendrick; PROD: Monja Danischewsky; SCR: Compton Mackenzie, Angus Macphail (from Mackenzie's novel); PHOT: Gerald Gibbs; MUS: Ernest Irving.

OSCAR NOMINATIONS: None. (Winner best film 1948: *Hamlet.*)

82 minutes. B&W

255

Wild Strawberries
Smultronstallet (1957)

Bergman made this and *The Seventh Seal* in the same year. They are two very different films and yet they complement each other in that each deals with a quest. In *The Seventh Seal*, the knight is looking for God; in *Wild Strawberries*, the elderly professor, on his way to receive an honorary degree, uses the journey to discover and understand himself and the effect he has had on others. The action covers past and present, reality and fantasy, the present harshly and starkly lit, the earlier memories more relaxed and lyrical as if, for an old man, the past – that other country – was better than the time and

place he inhabits now. Each new character, each reminiscence as it springs up in the professor's mind reveals something new about him – his failings, his shortcomings, the reasons why, in his apparently successful and honoured old age, he is alone and lonely. This is, admittedly, an uneven film, verbally overexplicit, but it is packed with vivid imagery – an early dream sequence, both mysterious and yet significant; a disenchanted couple squabbling fiercely in a car; the sad beauty of Ingrid Thulin, as the unhappy daughter-in-law; the distancing effect produced by the device of having the professor

The old professor (Victor Sjostrom) on a journey of disillusionment through his own past.

(Victor Sjostrom, splendid in his last screen role) visiting his own past unseen by those who shared it with him. It's a sombre, striking work, uncompromising in its examination of the protagonist. If *The Seventh Seal* showed Bergman to be a director of international stature, *Wild Strawberries* confirmed the diagnosis.

MAIN CAST: Victor Sjostrom, Ingrid Thulin, Gunnar Bjornstrand, Bibi Andersson, Naima Wifstrand, Jullan Kindahl, Max von Sydow. DIR/SCR: Ingmar Bergman; PROD: Allan Ekelund; PHOT: Gunnar Fischer; MUS: Erik Nordgren.

OSCAR NOMINATION: Best screenplay. (Winner best film 1959: *Ben-Hur*; winner best foreign language film: *Black Orpheus*.)

93 minutes. B&W. Swedish – subtitled

The Wizard Of Oz (1939)

Whether this is art is open to doubt; that it is a screen classic is unarguable. And what it seems to indicate is that classics, like art, can often be created not only by accident but against the odds. For consider: originally MGM wanted Shirley Temple to play Dorothy but 20th Century Fox wouldn't release her; Buddy Ebsen was cast as the Scarecrow, then swapped roles with the Tin Man (Ray Bolger), discovered he was allergic to the metallic paint and

was replaced by Jack Haley; Edna May Oliver, first choice for the Wicked Witch, gave way to Margaret Hamilton; two directors were involved – King Vidor for the sepia scenes at the beginning and end, Victor Fleming for the rest; and when the film was found to be too long, MGM had to be restrained from lopping out its most famous and most beloved song, 'Over the Rainbow'. Yet despite all this and some reviews that verged on the grudg-

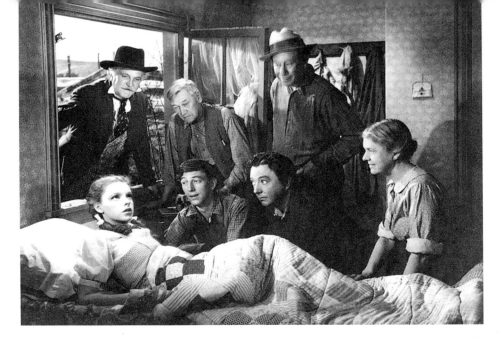

'Oh, Auntie Em, there's no place like home.' – Dorothy back in Kansas after her fantastical adventures in Oz.

ing, this fantastical story of a young girl and her dog, transplanted by a storm to the land of Oz and trying to get back to Kansas, remains the yardstick against which all other cinematic fairy tales must be measured. For sheer enchantment and magic none has surpassed it and, I submit, only *E.T.* has come close to matching it. A cartoon sequel, *Journey Back to Oz*, with Judy Garland's daughter Liza Minnelli providing the voice of Dorothy, was made in 1971; in 1978 Diana Ross starred in an all-black grown-up version called *The Wiz*; and there had been a silent film of *The Wizard of Oz* in 1925. The latter, lacking sound, was hardly in the same class and the other two can best be regarded as tributes, rather than rivals, to the 1939 picture.

MAIN CAST: Judy Garland, Ray Bolger, Jack Haley, Bert Lahr, Margaret Hamilton, Frank Morgan, Billie Burke, Charlie Grapewin, Clara Blandick. DIR: Victor Fleming (and King Vidor); PROD: Mervyn Le Roy; SCR: Noel Langley, Florence Ryerson, Edgar Allan Wolfe (from the book by Frank L. Baum); PHOT: Harold Rosson; MUS: Herbert Stothart; ART DIR: Cedric Gibbons, William A. Horning.

OSCARS: Best song ('Over the Rainbow' mus by Harold Arlen, lyr by E.Y. Harburg); best score (Stothart). OSCAR NOMINATIONS: Best film; best art direction; best special effects (A. Arnold Gillespie, Douglas Shearer). In addition, Garland was awarded a statuette for 'her outstanding performance as a screen juvenile during the past year'. (Winner best film 1939: *Gone with the Wind*.)

192 minutes. Colour and B&W

Z (1968)

Most political thrillers work only on one level. Either the thriller element is merely an excuse for the political message or vice versa. Z works on both. The story is based on a true incident – the murder in Greece in 1965 of a left-wing activist, who was knocked down by a truck as he left a peace meeting. In the film, Greece is not identified. Instead Z, played by Yves Montand, is the leader, eventually murdered, of an opposition pacifist group in an unnamed Mediterranean country. But in the film, as in fact, the investigation into the killing, conducted by Jean-Louis Trintignant, reveals widespread political corruption and intimidation. This is a classic example of the individual versus the State and a chilling examination of the way in which tyranny – in this case Fascist tyranny – can masquerade under the guise of law and order. As a condemnation of the then 'Colonels' regime' in Greece, Z was highly topical, but its concern with individual human rights, as pertinent now as it was then or indeed in any era, also lends it a timeless quality. The style of the film, occasionally over-restless and strident, may be of the 1960s, but the political message and warning it delivers should be heeded by every generation. And along with that goes an extremely well-wrought thriller which, never mind the film's other qualities, grabs and holds the attention. It's an unusual combination – a gripping popular entertainment, a taut, fast-moving melodrama, that also makes a serious and considered political statement. The film was made in France and Algeria and – a high com-

Z, based on the assassination of Grigoris Lambrakis, was Costa-Gavras's revenge on the right-wing Greek government that had blacklisted him.

pliment, this – was banned in Greece. Its themes of guilt and despotism have remained central to Costa-Gavra's work ever since and its immediate success, with cineastes and audiences alike, inevitably spawned – another high compliment – a host of imitators in Europe and America.

MAIN CAST: Yves Montand, Jean-Louis Trintignant, Irene Papas, Jacques Pérrin, François Périer, Charles Denner. DIR: Constantin Costa-Gavras; PROD: Jacques Pérrin, Hamed Rachedi; SCR: Costa-Gavras, Jorge Semprun (from the novel by Vassili Vassilikos); PHOT: Raoul Coutard; MUS: Mikis Theodorakis.

OSCAR (1969): Best foreign language film. OSCAR NOMINATIONS: Best film; best director; best screenplay; best film editing (Françoise Bonnot). (Winner best film 1969: *Midnight Cowboy*.)

123 minutes. Colour. French – subtitled

Illustrations Acknowledgements

The author and publisher would like to express their appreciation to the following for their assistance and/or permission to reproduce the photographs in this book:

ABC Television, British Film Institute, Columbia Pictures Corporation, Cinema International Corporation, Films de France, Katz Pictures, The Kobal Collection, London Features International, Photofest, Paramount Pictures Corporation, Pictorial Press Limited, The Rank Organisation, The Ronald Grant Archive, Seven Arts Inc., United Artists Corporation, 20th Century Fox, The Walt Disney Company Ltd., Warner Pathé.

Index

Index

Index

Index